PREDATORS
I HAVE KNOWN

Alan Dean Foster

OPEN ROAD

INTEGRATED MEDIA

NEW YORK

cover design by Jim Tierney
interior design by Danielle Young

ISBN: 978-1-4532-5825-5

Published in 2011 by Open Road Integrated Media
180 Varick Street
New York, NY 10014
www.openroadmedia.com

To Gaia

CONTENTS

INTRODUCTION   8

I   TYGER, TYGER, BURNING BRIGHT...   12
East Central India, April 2003

II   THINGS YOU NEVER FORGET   20
South Australia, January 1991

III   FELIX   38
Mount Etjo, Namibia, November 1993

IV   THE CUTE LITTLE OCTOPUS AND THE HOMICIDAL SHELL   48
East Central Australia, November 1989

V   JEALOUS ANTS, MILLIONS OF ANTS, AND REALLY, REALLY   58
BIG...ANTS
Southeastern Peru, May 1987
Northeastern Gabon, January 2007
Southeastern Peru, July 1998

VI   SHARKS I HAVEN'T JUMPED   80
Bismarck Sea, September 1997
West Australia, April 1992

VII   FLAT TIRES, OLD CANVAS, AND BIG CATS   98
Tanzania, July 1984
South Africa, May 2002
Tanzania, August 1984
Mount Etjo, Namibia, October 1993

VIII   MEANWHILE, SAFELY BACK HOME...   118
Prescott, Arizona, Anytime

IX   EYES ON THE TRAIL   134
Central Gabon, January 2007

X   EVER WONDER HOW *WE* TASTE?   144
Papua New Guinea, October 1995
Tanzania, July 1984
Southeastern Peru, May 1987: A Sartorial Digression

XI   EATING, YAWNING, AND COITUS INTERRUPTUS   158
Northern Botswana, October 1993

XII   AIR JAWS   170
South Africa, June 2002

XIII   DRACULA IS A MUTE   182
Northern Borneo, September 2010

XIV   TEENAGE KILLER NINJA OTTERS   190
Southwestern Brazil, May 2000

CONCLUSION   204

Born to water,
Live like fire,
Leave like the wind . . .

INTRODUCTION

OVER THE PAST FORTY YEARS, in the course of visiting six of the seven continents and a good portion of the world's seas, it has been my privilege to observe and marvel at thousands of different animals in their natural habitats. Every one of them, from leafhoppers to leeches, has been in one way or another fascinating, intriguing, and beautiful.

Still, there is no doubt that of all Earth's creatures we retain a special admiration for those bold enough, brave enough, and tough enough to contend with us on our own terms. So used are we to making food of every other living thing that when one comes along that is inclined—circumstances permitting—to make a meal of us, we are often struck dumb with admiration at the sheer audacity of it. Are not we humans the masters, the controllers, the lords and overseers of this world?

As civilized and populated as it has become, not always.

Thankfully, I say. Most of us live daily lives far too cosseted. Surrounded by the artifacts of our burgeoning, squalling, sprawling civilization, it is all too easy to lose touch with Nature and all that she proffers.

Sometimes she offers us contacts we would rather not make. When they occur, such moments, such encounters, offer us a charge, an exchange, a taste of something our ancestors knew intimately but we have largely forgotten. It is a good and useful thing to experience again such moments in time. At a suitable distance, of course.

Sometimes, the intervening space contracts, often when we least expect it to do so. Then the adrenaline surges, the pupils expand, the heart pumps a little (occasionally a lot) faster, and we feel more alive than usual. There is inestimable beauty in such encounters. At least, there is as long as you watch where you are stepping, or putting your hand, or focusing your eyes.

I write a fair amount of science fiction. If you think back on the stories you've read in that genre, or the films you've seen, some of the most powerful images (visual or literary) are those that feature beings that pose a physical threat to our existence. From H. G. Wells's *The War of the Worlds* to *Alien* and *Predator*, we savor the frisson of fear that comes with imagining there are things Out There that might find us edible, or at the very least would be pleased to extinguish our existence.

What many readers or moviegoers don't know is that such experiences are present right here on Earth, if one is willing to step outside the boundaries of the familiar and the comfortable and meet those experiences on their own territory. Often such an encounter, as with white sharks or tigers or poisonous snakes, will lead to straightforward renderings of these creatures in the tales I tell. Other times, they'll provide inspiration, a carnivorous springboard, to the invention of predators more alien and outré than those that actually live here on our home planet, as in books like *Midworld*, *Sentenced to Prism*, and the Journeys of the Catechist trilogy.

Step outside the boundaries of the familiar, I urge. Herewith some of the steps I have taken over the years; all memorable, all engraved permanently in my mind, all capable of reiterating that special charge of which I have written. None of them has resulted in any of the creatures described making a meal of all or part of me.

Yet.

Alan Dean Foster
Prescott, Arizona

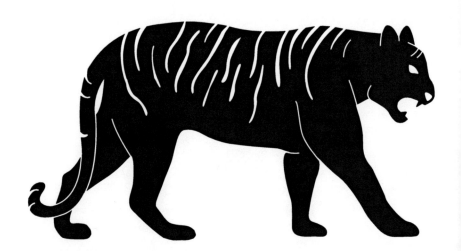

I

TYGER, TYGER, BURNING BRIGHT...

East Central India, April 2003

THEN THE TIGER SAW ME, and everything changed. The world looks different from the back of an elephant. Riding on a bench seat slung over the spine of an ambling elephant is akin to being on a very small but very stable ship in the midst of a choppy sea. There is more pitching than rolling, complicated by the fact that another rider is seated in close proximity to you on the other side of the perambulating pachyderm while the guiding mahout straddles the animal's neck sans saddle or any other tack. I thought it would be like riding a horse. It's not. Horses jolt and jounce you; elephants don't. Horses have style. Elephants have . . . mass.

We were patrolling the vast, hilly, uninhabited forest of Kanha National Park. Located in the eastern state of Madhya Pradesh, the nearly 800-square-mile Kanha has a reputation as the best-managed national park in India and forms the core of the Kanha Tiger Reserve. Here, in these rambling, rolling woods, Rudyard Kipling found his inspiration for the *Jungle Book* tales of the boy-cub Mowgli and of Baloo, Bagheera, and his other animal friends and enemies.

Far from the tourist-saturated haunts of Agra and Jaipur, not easy to reach from the great cities of Mumbai and Kolkata, the reserve's remoteness and lack of accessing infrastructure (i.e., terrible roads) ensures that it is one of the least visited national parks in the country. Bad for tour buses. Very good for tigers. And also for those who fervently desire to see one of the great cats outside the confines of a zoo or wild animal park and in its natural surroundings.

A tiger in a zoo is like a bucket of bright red paint dumped on an asphalt road. How, one wonders while marveling at the resplendent amalgam of orange body, black stripes, and white highlights, can it possibly sneak up on prey? Surely, such a boldly demarcated predator must stick out in the wild as plainly as it does in front of our moat-and-railing shielded selves? What more blatant a four-legged banner, what more sharply defined a feline body from whiskers to tail, exists on the planet? Why, it's impossible to *avoid* seeing it!

But put it in its thick native forests of sal and bamboo, in the depths of the surroundings for which it has evolved, and the tiger vanishes. Hundreds of pounds of carnivorous cat become as difficult to see as a dispersing wisp of orange smoke. The tiger does not dwell in the dark steaming greenhouse of cheap jungle films. It thrives in dry woods of brown and yellow, of broken patterns and shattered shade where tree blends into bush, bush into rock, and rock into shadow. You can gaze directly at one of the great meat eaters from a short distance away and still not see it.

The tiger is patient. The tiger knows how to wait. Nature does not make mistakes when she is handing out camouflage.

It had been a fine, lazy morning, replete with sightings of creatures as common as the crow and as rare as the jungle cat. Foraging chitals and sambars roam the hills and plains of Kanha. Wild boars snuffle unseen in its capillary network of narrow gullies. Blue-bellied rollers and green barbets flash between trees like strips of metallic foil riding the wind. Gaurs, a kind of wild cattle, loll near small streams or in mud wallows. The distinctive call of the muntjac, or barking deer, crackles through the forest.

Most impressively, Kanha is where the barasinghas have made their last stand. From a single surviving group of sixty-six, the Kanha herd of these striking swamp deer now numbers in the hundreds—a rare success story in a world of declining species and shrinking habitat.

Lulled into a semi-somnamublistic state by the heat and the steady, monotonous plodding of our patient elephant, I didn't see the tiger until our excited mahout quietly pointed it out, and then I had to look twice. The powerful, muscular two-year-old male was relaxing on his belly to the left of a tree, as inconspicuous and hard to pick out as one of its roots. He was not trying to hide. He didn't have to try. Nature took care of that for him. Had it not been for the sharp and experienced eyes of the mahout, we would have ambled right past without detecting him.

Now that I knew where to look, however, I could see it clearly. How could I possibly have missed it before? The cat was huge, between 300 and 400 pounds of pure predatory power at rest. Stripes blending into coat. Coat seeping into trees and bush and rocks. I immediately found myself mesmerized by two particular components of this magnificent representative of the order Felidae. It was not so much that I *wanted* to focus on them. They compelled me to do so. I found myself inexorably drawn to them.

They were the eyes and the teeth.

At the moment, the eyes were inclined upward. Tracking the arc of a bird, perhaps, or checking some suggestive rustling in the branches overhead. The deceptively soft mouth was open as the tiger, panting, sought relief from the midday heat. The exposed canines—they were longer than my middle finger—bright and gleaming and perfectly white, as if their owner had just had them cleaned by a local dentist. Reposing in the cooling shade as if fully aware of his own inescapable majesty, thick tongue flopping, massive body heaving slightly, he was just as I might have imagined him: all barely contained brawn and quiet magnificence. Then, almost absently, he lowered his eyes and looked straight at me. We locked. This is what his eyes said, accentuated with mild interest and palpable speculation.

I can kill you if I want.

In that instant, my tiger looked something other than magnificent. A connection had been made as piercingly and effectively as if I had stuck a finger into a wall socket. It was not the first time a glance from a carnivore had made me feel like meat, but it was the first time I had sensed genuine contemplation behind the look: calculation in addition to evaluation.

I can kill you if I want.

That stare shrank the distance between us as effectively as a fold in space-time. Though I had been told that the tiger would consider me as part of the elephant atop which I fortunately was riding, I no longer felt completely at ease. My belly was calm and relaxed, but mentally the relationship between the cat and I had undergone a radical change. I *knew* what that gaze meant. Knew instinctively. Remembered it from thousands of years of my forebears having been torn apart and consumed by long-dead relatives of what had instantly morphed into something far more immediate and visceral than a singular tourist attraction.

Having silently and effortlessly made his point, the tiger casually returned his attention to whatever had drawn his gaze into the tree's upper branches. We lingered and watched for a while; taking pictures, searing the sight into memory, and then moved on.

That was it, I thought as I remembered to breathe again. I'd had my tiger sighting. What I had come all this way over thousands of miles and along horrific roads in order to hopefully encounter had, at last, thankfully and admirably, if somewhat unsettlingly, presented itself to my captivated eyes. The elephant moved on, and I counted myself fortunate.

The mahout angled us downward into a steep-sided dry gully barely two elephants wide. Fringed with dense forest on both banks, it offered an easy, unobstructed path back to camp for our patient, bamboo-munching mount. I had put away my video camera and was contemplating imminent relief from the increasing heat and humidity when my Indian friend Negi suddenly cried out, "He's coming out! The tiger is coming out!"

In the clammy, cloying sweat that coated my face, my body, my head, and trickled unstoppably into my burning eyes, I found myself confused. What did that mean: "He's coming out!"? My slightly addled, humidity-sodden mind confused contemporary urban concerns with actual immediacies. Was the tiger gay? "Coming out" of what? Out of where? It finally struck me. The tiger was coming out of the forest. But we were traveling below surface level along the bottom of the desiccated wash. So that must mean . . .

There is not much room to maneuver on the sloping back of an elephant; less so for someone unaccustomed to that ancient but eclectic mode of transport. Seating consists of a pair of simple, open wooden benches slung like saddlebags over the elephant's back. One person sits on one side, a second on the other, with the mahout straddling the elephant's neck.

"He's coming out. He's coming out!" Negi's voice was rising with his excitement.

My gear. Where the hell was my gear? I groped for the video camera, then for the battery. Fumbling to put them together was like trying to forcibly mate a pair of reluctant spiders. I could not see what was behind me. If I turned too fast and dropped the camera, it would shatter. (It is a surprisingly long way from the top of an elephant to the ground.) If I dropped the battery, the camera would be useless in my hands. If I was too careless or too hasty in my efforts, I might lose my balance and fall off myself. Then the tiger would no longer see me as part of the elephant, and something Really Bad might happen. In the bumbling confusion and frantic rush to get the camera working, I chanced a complete twist of my upper body in order to snatch a hasty look behind me. The young male had indeed come out of the forest and was once more looking at us.

Down at us.

The tiger was standing on the edge of the gully's right bank. Framed by trees and sky, he presented as glorious an image as one could possibly imagine. Edgar Rice Burroughs could not have positioned him better. Now out of the shade and standing in full sunlight, he gleamed beneath the baking Indian sun like living, breathing sculpture: pure untrammeled ferocity held barely in check. It was as if he had decided, in the course of his casual inspection of the strange multiheaded creature ambling along just ahead of and below him, to strike a deliberately dominating pose.

Camera—battery—clumsy human digits uncoordinated. As I tried to work faster, it occurred to me.

The tiger was looking *down* at me. That meant he was higher than the back of an elephant. Higher, and very, very near. He would not even have to exert himself. Half a pounce and he would be on top of the elephant. On top of . . . me. As this realization struck home, an odd heaviness passed through my gut, as if I had ingested a chunk of cold iron.

The moment passed. Deciding he had better things to do, the tiger turned and sauntered nonchalantly back into the shadowy dry forest, his swaying backside essaying a tango, his tail switching back and forth like the taunting lure at the end of a fishing pole. Ready at last, I aimed the camera—and proceeded to acquire some excellent video of disturbed twigs and rustling leaves.

Sometimes, in the dark of night, when I lie in bed at home with the television off and my wife calm and asleep beside me, I close my eyes just a little, and I can experience once again that moment of predator-and-prey eye contact as precise and clear as when it occurred in the baking forest of Kanha. So beautiful. So unique. And not a little soul-shivering.

I can kill you if I want.

II

THINGS YOU NEVER FORGET

South Australia, January 1991

THERE ARE SOME THINGS IN life that never escape your memory no matter how much your other reminiscences fade. Your first date. Your first love. If you are an artist or musician or writer, your first sale. Your first home of your own.

Your first great white shark.

Tellers of tall tales have been inventing inimical creatures since before Frankenstein. Rocs and griffins. Dragons and centaurs. In the course of forty years of writing, I've concocted one or two myself. While research-ing the impossible for your fiction, you inevitably come across the most extreme examples of what our own planet has actually produced. In today's increasingly civilized, urbanized, Internet-connected world, there are not many creatures that we fear might actually eat us—the fear of being eaten alive being among humankind's oldest terrors. Among these more ominous representatives of the animal kingdom, *Carcharodon car-charias* occupies a place very close to the ultimate.

Carcharodon is not the largest predator in the sea. That honor belongs to the sperm whale, *Physeter macrocephalus*. Next in size comes the orca, or killer whale. But save for rutting bulls, sperm whales are easygoing leviathans whose principal interest lies in consuming large, soft squid rather than tiny, bony humans. Meanwhile, show business has Shamu-ed the orca into a cuddly giant squeaky toy not dissimilar from an oversize black-and-white seagoing puppy.

Furthermore, there are no confirmed records of a sperm whale or an orca deliberately attacking and killing a human being in order to eat it, whereas *Carcharodon* has been known, however mistakenly, to make a meal out of the occasional human swimmer, surfer, or spearfisher. The great white generates an atavistic fear in humans no dozen whales come close to matching. The fact that it is also a stealth hunter only adds to the terror it engenders. It is the oceanic equivalent of the clutching hand in a horror movie reaching out from the dark to grab the unsuspecting victim from behind.

As a writer hoping to invent terrifying aliens and ravening otherworldly monsters, I reasoned, it would behoove me to take stock of the nearest actual equivalent the earth has to offer. While it's easy enough to go to the zoo and observe land-based carnivores, the distancing that results, the presence of moats and heavy bars separating observer from the observed, strongly mitigates against the intensity of the experience. Not to mention the fact that most of the time the imprisoned lions and tigers and bears—oh my—seem utterly disinterested in their eager human visitors. In contrast, I had read that the great white shark tends not to be disinterested in those humans who dare to immerse themselves in its element. Quite the contrary. In January 1991, I set off for the wild coast of South Australia to find out.

At the hotel in Sydney, my fellow expedition members had already begun to arrive. I looked forward to meeting them with more than casual interest, since it was not inconceivable that at some point in the immediate future my continued well-being and/or my life might depend on their respective underwater skills and good judgment.

The first to appear was Brent Mills, youthful scion of a famous family-run portrait photography company based in Chattanooga, Tennessee. Brent was open, cheerful, and friendly, like an overgrown Boy Scout who had been blessed with an outsized allowance. His home back in Chattanooga looked like a bombed-out Kodak warehouse, overflowing with more photographic bells, whistles, and gewgaws than I imagine could exist in the feverish dreams of any would-be Ansel Adams.

Next to say hello was Dr. Michael Fritsch of Indianapolis. Mike was quiet, charming, and afflicted with the slightly far-off look of one for whom work is never done. He had, in fact, actually brought with him work to do on the second medical book he was preparing. I would have had someone to discuss writing with, if not for the fact that half the contents were probably in Latin and far beyond my layman's ken. Considering that he was far from pushing forty, I was much impressed with what he had managed to accomplish in such a short period of time.

Carl Roessler appeared. One of the world's great underwater photographers, he was a peripatetic, athletic fifty-seven-year-old brimming with the energy and enthusiasm of a man doing exactly what he wanted to do in life. He had the demeanor and face of a mischievous imp and the skin tone of a cosseted Irishman. Out on the open water the unforgiving Aussie sun would tend to fry him, and he knew it. Despite the very real risk of skin cancer, he regularly visited equatorial climes in search of new dive sites and better pictures. Such was the dedication of the devoted diver and wizened photographer.

Greg Sindmack was an obstetrician from Riverside, California. If he cared for the newborns he delivered with the same intensity he did his camera gear, then expectant mothers under his supervision had nothing to worry about. He also cussed more than any physician I'd ever met.

While during the short but bouncy flight from Sydney to Adelaide, Greg and I sweated over the state of our camera gear; Carl, Mike, and Brent experienced no such concerns because they sensibly traveled with specialized photo-equipment travel luggage strong enough to stop an antitank missile.

Arriving in Adelaide, we met up with Sebastian Horseley, the last paying member of our expedition. Sebastian was an English artist of unfamiliar reputation and intense iconoclasm. He promptly began hurling questions at everyone with the speed and facility of a ninja flinging throwing stars. Of himself, he said little. In dress, he inclined to black accented by the occasional outrageous T-shirt. Gradually, we winkled out of him the information that he had only just learned to dive during a recent visit to Thailand. This, therefore, was to be only his second experience with scuba. We eyed one another and shrugged. It's his life.

The charming fishing town of Port Lincoln likes to be known as Tunarama City, after the annual tuna celebration that's held there every year: a sort of rural piscine Mardi Gras. The bucolic little town of some 12,000 souls is located an hour's flight west of Adelaide on the opposite side of the vast Spencer Gulf. Beyond Port Lincoln lie only towns barely large enough to rate a mention on a map, and the vast Nullarbor Plain—a perfectly flat, virtually featureless section of the globe that makes the American Great Plains look like Switzerland. The Nullarbor runs all the way across the continent nearly to the shores of the Indian Ocean. We were met at Port Lincoln's minimalist airport by our host and guide, Rodney Fox, and his strapping son, Andrew.

On December 8, 1963, while competing for his third consecutive title in the Australian National Spearfishing Championships, Rodney Fox was nearly bitten in half by a great white shark. Every rib on the left side of his body was crushed, one tooth pierced his clavicle clean through, and it took 452 stitches to close up the great wound in his side. When he finally arrived at the local hospital, there was so little blood left in his body that his veins would have collapsed, had five more minutes elapsed before transfusions commenced.

Since that near-death encounter, Fox has made the study of the great white his lifework. In the years since the attack, he has guided scientists and researchers, game specialists and professional photographers on regular expeditions to study the most elusive and mesmerizing carnivore in the sea. He'll even take along the odd, compulsively curious writer.

Rodney turned out to be a tall, soft-spoken chap with a quick smile, thinning hair, and a perpetual twinkle in his eye. He looked like the staff member Kris Kringle would have had to keep putting on administrative leave for playing too many practical jokes on the other elves. Having collaborated on this trip many times previously, he and Carl immediately began swapping jokes and greetings and old stories. Son Andrew proved to be much quieter, almost shy, and bigger, with the stalwart build of a football lineman.

Accompanying them was Jack Bellamy, who would comprise one-third of our ship's crew. The blue-collar third. The one who does the dirty work. He was tall, limber, and bore a perfectly uncanny resemblance to a certain mythical sailor inordinately fond of spinach, except he had no pipe clenched between his teeth. His strine (Aussie dialect) was thicker than that of a beer-soaked koala. The rest of us nonetheless managed communication without benefit of a translator.

The picturesque Port Lincoln harbor was home to a number of pleasure craft and numerous hardworking fishing boats. Since the Japanese, Koreans, Taiwanese, and Mainland Chinese had joined the locals in seriously depleting the area's tuna, these boats had turned to catching shrimp and other fish. Abalone and crayfish (or crays, a kind of slipper lobster) are also profitably taken in the nearby waters.

Far from being a luxury vessel, the boat for our expedition, the *Nenad*, was a working shrimper, identical to the craft you see in those oversize photos that decorate the walls of every Red Lobster restaurant. Two shark cages secured atop an open platform above the rear deck constituted exceptions to the typical shrimping gear. One was fashioned from aluminum, the other steel. Each was about six feet square by seven tall, with twin cylindrical metal float tanks welded to the top and a horizontal camera port encircling the entire cage at shoulder level. This unbarred opening was at least a foot high. Everyone's silent gaze was drawn immediately to the place where there were no protective bars. The gap looked bigger than I imagined it might be.

Joining up with us in Port Lincoln along with Sebastian Horseley were Klaus and Renate Reith from Stuttgart, a delightful couple in their mid-thirties who made their living as professional photographers and multimedia show presenters. Their arrival led to an entirely unforeseen difficulty. It seems they had brought their daughter along with them. This, in itself, was not a problem. The problem arose from the fact that their daughter was . . . five.

Presented with this potential fait accompli, a clearly troubled Carl and Rodney caucused. They then asked the opinion of the rest of us. We eyed one another uneasily. The gist of our conclusion was that what to do and how to proceed was not for us to say. I mumbled something about adequate insurance. Someone made the inevitable unseemly joke about five-year-olds being just the right size to serve as shark bait.

The Reiths had traveled farther and spent more than anyone else in order to participate in the expedition. Bearing this in mind, everyone reluctantly swallowed their concerns and agreed they could come along.

As we started to load the *Nenad*, out of dark depths redolent not of orcs but of prawns burst an Australian-Slav hobbit named Mateo Ricov. Swarthy, ebullient Captain Ricov looked exactly like one of the Greek resistance fighters from *The Guns of Navarone*. I peered past him, but Anthony Quinn and Gregory Peck were nowhere to be seen. As we prepared to depart, Mateo was everywhere, loudly and enthusiastically attending to last-minute details.

Also making an appearance at this time was Silvy Slausen, our cook. In her early twenties, affable and attractive, she was to be one of only two women on board a small boat for eight days with twelve men. I could not but admire her self-assurance. The bachelors among us admired her even more, until everyone was tactfully but in no uncertain terms informed that she was the fiancée of the very large and perhaps not altogether shy Andrew Fox.

After much picture taking, the *Nenad*'s sturdy diesels were fired up and we headed out to sea.

A pounding, rolling, all-day journey found us approximately a hundred miles from the mainland, rocking in the lee of the small, isolated, and uninhabited North Neptune Islands. Once clear of Port Lincoln, we sighted not a single other craft, not even on the *Nenad*'s radar. We were bobbing in the body of cold water known as the Great Australian Bight, and the next substantial chunk of dry land due south of our position was Antarctica. The weather was windy, overcast, and cold, most unusual for this part of the world in mid-January. Knowing it was exceptional was small consolation to those of us who had traveled halfway around the world in hopes of clear skies and warm sunshine.

Despite the stabilizers that had been added for the benefit of visiting landlubbers like ourselves, the *Nenad* bobbed and weaved like Lee Marvin's horse in *Cat Ballou*. Dr. Fritsch was immediately seasick, and would remain wretchedly so for the majority of the voyage. He spent a great deal of time in his bunk, stomaching (if one dare visualize) his unhappy situation in stoic silence. Others endured the rough conditions to greater or lesser degree. Renate Reith endured the discomfort in despondent German. My knowledge of the language not being up to fully comprehending the full extent of her suffering, the perfectly bilingual Fritsch helpfully translated the details of her ongoing misery for the rest of us.

Soothing our souls as well as our stomachs, Silvy extracted gourmet meals from hidden closets and drawers. She appeared to use recipes, but I'm convinced magic was involved. With varying degrees of enthusiasm, the non-sufferers among us wolfed down these wondrous meals three times a day. A huge cooler designed to hold ice to preserve the regular shrimp catch overflowed with iced sodas and beer. As the only teetotaler aboard, the others were delighted by my disinterest, which left that much more XXXX and Foster's Lager for them. Alas, there was nothing comparable in consumables for which to trade my allotted ration of grog.

The North Neptune Islands consist of several small, craggy, granitic scabs protruding not far above the chilly waves. Like most of the islands out in the bight, they are barren and seldom visited. The larger of the two provided some shelter for our rocking craft as well as a safe haven for an assortment of wandering seabirds, determined low scrub, and hundreds if not thousands of barking, moaning, wheezing, bellowing, stinking New Zealand fur seals. It was the calving season, and the great slick wet arc of black boulder-strewn shoreline was a jumbled rookery crammed with squalling pups the size of overfed poodles.

We went ashore to photograph and observe, able to approach the unconcerned and rarely visited animals to within touching distance, discovering that the pups will nip at your fingers if you're not careful. They are utterly captivating little critters. Their presence in considerable numbers was also the reason the *Nenad* had anchored offshore their nursery.

Pinnipeds are the great white's favorite prey, and the younger and less experienced, the easier they are to catch. This feeding preference holds true wherever great whites are to be found, from Australia to South Africa to the shores of central California.

Back on board, Rodney, Jack Bellamy, and Andrew were busily dishing out the chum. Consisting of blood, fish oil, and fish parts, the chum, or shark lure, was compiled according to a special recipe of Rodney's own devising. I expected the gory concoction to reek to high heaven, but, oddly, it hardly smelled at all. This lack of pungency might have been a side benefit of the cool weather. Ladled or hosed overboard, the dark slick was swiftly carried out to the open sea by the steady current. The reaction a shark has to crossing a chum line approximates that of a blond forty-year-old multiple divorcée encountering the naive male heir to a modest fortune. It garners immediate attention.

But great whites are wary, unpredictable creatures. The pre-expedition literature repeatedly warned that despite the crew's best efforts to attract them, it was entirely possible we might not encounter any at all. In 1990, six of the expedition's allotted eight days elapsed before a single shark put in an appearance, and only two sharks were seen altogether.

Chaining our impatience, we settled down to wait. The literature and Carl's judicious admonitions prepared us. We had books, games, diving and photographic equipment to see to, in addition to well-packed layers of patience. We were quite prepared to linger at the site for as long as it might take our quarry to arrive.

Exactly one hour and forty-five minutes after dropping anchor, Captain Ricov was heard singing out, *"Shark!"*

There ensued a mad scramble to vacate our constipated below-deck quarters the likes of which I have not experienced since I was in the army and it was announced that the mess hall that night was serving steak. Everyone rushed—no, rocketed—to the *Nenad*'s stern.

In the dark green-black water astern, two fins. The mind registers, evaluates, then corrects. No. One fin, one tail, both belonging to the same impossibly large fish. We gawked, entranced, at the water as though a vision from the Cretaceous had magically appeared before us. We were not far wrong.

Advancing with effortless, leisurely sweeps of its huge scythelike tail, the great white slipped casually through the chum to pass with utter indifference less than a yard from the stern. As it did so, it rolled onto its left side to eye us. That pupilless jet-black eye is like nothing else I have seen in Nature. As the shark opened its mouth, we were permitted a glimpse of dentition, a flash of pure white enamel whose individual components were triangular in shape and serrated like steak knives.

The shark dropped out of sight, and we discovered that we had all been holding our breath. A few moments later, it returned and began to circle the boat. It was a youngster, not very big, perhaps only nine feet long and weighing mere hundreds of pounds.

Andrew, Rodney, and Jack were in motion, setting out half tunas or mackerels secured to the ends of thin lines. These bleeding baits were put out to lure the shark in and keep it intrigued. To prevent the chunks of fish from sinking, ordinary colored balloons were attached to the bait lines. Bobbing up and down on the surface of a glassy and suddenly threatening sea, the cheap, brightly hued inflatable spheres were an incongruous sight in view of what was lurking in the water just beneath them.

Rodney informed us that the shark must take the bait or it would quickly lose interest and swim off. We waited and stared. Time passed— too much time.

Then a fin cut close, cut away, returned. A pointed nose momentarily cleaved the water, and the drifting hunk of fish vanished, the tough bait line snipped as easily as by scissors. Andrew hauled it in, its balloon float still attached and unharmed.

An hour later, a second shark appeared and took some bait. Carl was ecstatic, disbelieving. Two sharks the first day, almost within an hour of anchoring! Unbelievable. Rodney nodded, turned to us, and smiled.

"Anyone for a swim?"

That is what I traveled 8,000 miles for. That is why I've read science fiction since I was ten years old. The great shark is Van Vogt and Heinlein and Clarke become reality. It's Sheckley and Russell and Vance. But it is not fiction, not words on paper. The fantastic has been made flesh and given mass and color and alien patterns of its own.

In minutes, I had donned my heavy neoprene wet suit. Because the cages float on the surface, we would be working and observing in only eight feet of water. In full cold-water suit, that meant forty pounds of lead on the weight belt secured around my waist, or else I'd float to the top of the cage and bob up and down as helpless as an unpowered blimp. Between the weights and the tank on my back, I felt about as agile as a ruptured hippo. Trying to maintain my balance, I lurched toward the stern, staggering like Kharis the mummy.

The open top of the cage gaped invitingly. Hanging tightly to the gunwale, I stepped over the stern and pivoted laboriously. At that point, I found myself standing on the slippery eighteen-inch-wide diving platform that had been crudely fashioned from welded-together one-inch-diameter steel pipes. Cold water lapped over my feet and booties. (There is no need for fins within a shark cage.) With disconcerting irregularity, the swells caused the stern to dip down, the cage to surge up, and vice versa, never in tandem. If I mistimed my jump into the cage, I could hit the metal bars and break something—or miss it altogether. I looked around, my peripheral vision severely constrained by my mask. Where were the sharks? Were they watching me? Was I *their* fiction made real?

There was no time for anthropomorphizing. Others crowded the deck behind me, anxious and awaiting their turn. I was the first to step forward, and I was holding up the increasingly restless procession. *What the devil am I doing here?* The hell with it. Putting a hand over my face mask to keep it from being pushed off, I stepped out and down.

Into an instant Jacuzzi. A mad froth of bubbles exploded around me, obscuring my vision. My booted feet slammed into the grillwork bottom of the cage. A hasty check of my regulator showed that it was working fine, feeding me air from my tank, and I hoped I was not breathing too fast. Moving clear of the overhead opening, I grasped the metal webwork of the cage and dug my toes into the open bottom in order to steady myself upright in the rocking current. My head swiveled wildly.

There was no need. It was right there, coasting like a heavy bomber flying in slow motion, half obscured by the poor visibility and dark water. I heard the rush of bubbles and felt the momentary displacement as another diver entered the cage behind me, but I didn't turn to look in his direction or check his condition. I was intoxicated beyond words by what I was seeing—an awkward condition for a writer.

The shark turned and came around for a leisurely look at this new bait. Heading straight at you, a great white shark flashes the most unexpected and perverse frozen smile, sort of a cross between Bela Lugosi and the Cheshire Cat. Porpoises also possess a natural smile. This was different. *Carcharodon* sits at the top of the food chain and knows it. Warm-blooded it may be, but it's no mammal.

I realized that I was being inspected and evaluated as potential food.

The nine-foot shark looked twice as big underwater as it did from the safety and perspective of the *Nenad*'s deck. In the half-open mouth, teeth gleamed, each one as sharp as a double-edged razor. No other shark, no other living creature has teeth like that. The extinct *Tyrannosaurus rex* did. You can describe but not amplify upon them. A newspaper ad for a special shark exhibit at the Los Angeles County Museum of Natural History may have said it best: "Come see the first Cuisinart."

There is nothing flip, nothing frilly about the great white. Unlike many fish, it is neither gaudy nor brightly colored. It does not choose to advertise its remarkableness. In *Charcarodon*'s case, Nature has seen no need to elaborate, no justification for adding meretricious physical adjectives. Unlike fictional monsters with their horns and frills and iridescent hues, the great white is all business. Any drama inherent in its appearance is incidental to its single-minded task of feeding.

The shark gently bumped the cage with its snout and turned away, gliding weightlessly past. Reaching out, I let the tips of my fingers caress it as it swam by. "It's perfectly safe to touch them," Rodney had told us, adding without a hint of irony, "Just wait for the mouth to go past." The flesh and skin feels much like the unyielding head of a rubber mallet. Not rough at all. I started to extend my arm to try and grab the tail, then remembered the presence of the other shark and quickly drew my hand back into the cage.

For two days, we dove and marveled and photographed. The weather remained uncooperative; the seas rough. One night, I stood a two-hour watch alone on the stern deck as thousands of foot-long cream-white squid darted and shot through the water around the boat, attracted by its spotlights. The sharks were out there, too, making regular passes astern, the eeriness of their presence magnified by the silence and the darkness and the starry void overhead. I was transported as if to another world.

On the third day, it started to get crowded.

By the end of the fourth day, there were six great white sharks circling the *Nenad*, feeding and snapping, biting at the cages, at the divers within, at the boat and the bait. The inch-thick ropes that tethered the cages to the boat were repeatedly bitten through, severed as cleanly as if by a headsman's ax. The sharks nudged the cages. They gnawed at them. They slammed into them, all in vain attempts to get at the possibly tasty bipedal morsels they could see hovering within. Rodney avowed these were the most aggressive great whites he'd ever seen. We were too euphoric to be apprehensive.

Sebastian, our novice, stayed in the center of the cage and clung like a determined spider to the upper bars, as far away from the sharks as possible. Meanwhile, the rest of us obtained some of the most incredible still and video footage of sharks feeding and attacking.

The sharks were uncannily silent in their approach. One time, I sat down on the floor of the cage to check my camera, only to be told later by Klaus Reith that as I was doing so, a 2,000-pound, fourteen-foot female great white was nibbling intently at the bars not an arm's length directly behind my just-out-of-reach head.

I never heard it, and I never saw it. Great white: the stealth shark. Did *Tyrannosaurus rex* similarly lie in wait to ambush its prey?

Having singled out a victim, the great white charges, bites, and then retreats and circles. Seals and sea lions have sharp teeth and claws, so the shark waits for its flailing prey to bleed to death or expire from shock. Only then does it move in and feed. It was this precise behavior that likely saved Rodney Fox's life on that dreadful December day in 1963. The shark bit him and backed off, waiting for his life to seep away. Only his wet suit, acting like a giant Ace bandage, held him and his insides together long enough for him to reach the hospital.

You think of these things when you're in the water with half a dozen great whites, the largest of which Rodney estimated to be more than fifteen feet and 2,500 pounds. The biggest he's ever seen in nearly thirty years of diving with them was more than eighteen feet long—when he was assisting on the filming of the live-action shark sequence for the movie *Jaws*.

A fifteen-foot great white is much, much bigger than the cage. When its jaws are open to their greatest gape while taking some bait, its mouth becomes a small reddish cavern about a yard in diameter. If it's coming toward you, you can see right down its throat, past the gills. It looks like a small railroad tunnel, black and bottomless at the far end.

One day, the instant Carl jumped in to join me, a great white slammed into the cage in hopes of intercepting him, and by sheer coincidence, jammed its snout right through the unbarred camera port. With astonishing presence of mind born of a lifetime spent in the sea, Carl whirled around at this most disorienting moment of entry and gave the shark a couple of friendly pats on the nose with his gloved hands. At once fascinated and aghast, I observed this performance from the far side of the cage. Fortunately, the camera portal was large enough for the shark to partially enter but too small for it to open its mouth once it had its head partly inside. Tail churning the water to foam, it furiously backed out. Carl's mouth smiled around the edges of his regulator, his eyes twinkling with delight. Once again, I had to remind myself to breathe properly.

Days and sharks slid past. Having taken a dive interval, I was ready to return to the cage. Old stuff now to a veteran like myself. Routine. But there were three divers in the cage, and it was difficult for all of them to crowd far enough to one side to allow me ingress. I waited while Mateo repeatedly prodded one of the divers with a boat gaff to get them to move over. With weights and tank, I struggled to keep my balance on a choppy sea. Stepping down onto the diving platform, I found it increasingly difficult to maintain my equilibrium. I jumped.

My timing was bad.

A tremendous pain shot through my side, as though I'd just tried to run through the Pittsburg Steelers defensive line. Gasping in surprise and discomfort, I sank feetfirst to the bottom of the cage. My side was numb. As the shock of the initial impact began to wear off, the pain returned. Misjudging my entry, I had slammed my left side into the inch-thick center roof-support bar of the cage. This length of metal was intended to withstand the impact of flailing two-ton sharks without crumpling. It did not yield an iota to me.

I straightened and gingerly felt of my side where I'd hit. Contact made the pain no worse. I knew I should have signaled for help and aborted the dive, but I could not bring myself to do it. If something was seriously wrong, I might not be allowed another dive. With this foolish decision ruling my actions, I became aware that my mask was slowly flooding. The impact caused by my lousy entry had doubtless loosened something. I recalled my dive training. Keep calm; in the ocean, panic is the greatest danger.

Laboriously, I cleared my mask. It steadily refilled with cold salt water. I repeated the clearing procedure three, four times. Finally, I yanked off my wet-suit hood and angrily shoved my hair back. That solved the problem. The next time I cleared my mask, it stayed sealed. Meanwhile, I was losing heat through my exposed head, but I didn't care. At least, now I could see.

I spent valuable airtime rechecking myself and my camera. The latter seemed to have survived my awkward entry without damage. While this was transpiring, one by one the other divers were exiting the cage. It was lunchtime, I knew, and I was hungry, too, but I was damned if after all I had gone through I was going to climb out without seeing anything. Readying my camera and myself, I did a slow scan of the surrounding water. There were sharks everywhere.

I suddenly realized that I was entirely alone.

The other cage bobbed nearby in the current, empty. Moving faster than at any time since the start of the trip, I spun around in my own cage.

Likewise empty. And just like that, suddenly and unexpectedly, everything changed.

I was alone in the cold, cold water of the great Southern Ocean with half a dozen great white sharks.

The stern of the *Nenad* was twenty feet away. Only a pair of ropes connected my cage to it. For the first time since the first dive, the distance seemed more like half a mile even though I knew the longer distance was all in my head. Ninety feet below me, the sea bottom was invisible. And all around me, effortlessly circling, were the great whites.

I knew nothing could go wrong. I knew that they couldn't bite through the bars or break into the cage. I knew I had plenty of air, and that at any time I could open the cage's hinged roof and signal for help. Unless everyone was inside eating lunch (no, surely not!). My calm and rational self-reassurances did nothing to calm my abruptly altered emotional state. Now that I was alone in the water, all was different, strange, wonderful, and frightening.

This must be what the solitary Cro-Magnon hunter felt while huddling within his temporary shelter listening to the saber-toothed tigers and dire wolves howling outside, I thought. It is not an easy feeling to convey. There is a heightened sense of awareness. Every sense seems suddenly much sharper. You try to see every which way at once. Experiencing this, I was exalted. I was fearful. I was very much alive.

I shot footage like mad, swinging my video camera in all directions. For the first time, I had the whole cage to myself. There were no other divers to worry about or stumble in front of my lens. I moved freely as the sharks bit the cage, bumped it, tried to nibble off my toes. I was the food, and we both knew it, but it didn't matter. They were grand and beautiful as they swept past, unutterably regal in their power and strength. And for twenty-five minutes, they were all mine.

I was recording one biting the cage when I heard a distinct, sharp snap, like a dry tree branch breaking. A small bright white object appeared at the corner of my vision, tumbling through the water as the shark slid raggedly off the side of the cage. It was a tooth. Not a very big one. A small side tooth. Earlier, I had queried Carl about the possibility of obtaining such a souvenir.

"No one's ever gotten a tooth," he told me patiently. "I nearly did once. Grabbed at it three times, and had to watch it spin away through the floor of the cage. Wanted to cry."

You can't grab small things underwater. The faster and harder you clutch at them, the more water you push in front of your hand and the farther away goes the object you're trying to grab. As I futilely willed time to slow down, my thoughts raced madly: *Let go of the camera; let it go!* But the camera held all the underwater footage I'd taken and was buoyant enough in its EWA housing to rise swiftly upward and break against the bars if I let it out of my grasp.

So I held on to the camera housing while with my free hand I flailed forlornly at the rapidly descending tooth. Like a jitterbugging imp, it danced maddeningly around my fingertips while keeping well clear of actual contact. I forced myself to clutch at it more slowly. No matter. The current was helping it along; like a child's runaway top, it continued to pirouette swiftly downward, mocking me all the way. I took another futile swipe, knocking it slightly sideways.

Gone, I told myself. Now you know another reason why nobody's ever emerged from a dive with one of these.

The tooth struck the bottom support bar—and teetered there, caught between the grillwork floor and the outside.

Hardly breathing, I knelt and slowly extended my thumb and forefinger. The cage rocked back and forth in the surface current. My hand seemed an alien appendage, my fingers clumsy tools, the whole primate apparatus a clunky crane fit only for shifting boulders. My fingers closed around the tooth and contracted. I didn't care if I cut myself.

I had it.

Holding it up before my mask, I gazed at my prize in wonderment. It was all of an inch long. There the serrated edges, there the sharp point. Just like in the flat, dead book illustrations. Unlike in such illustrations, however, small bits of white flesh hung from the root. There was blood on the left side. Great white shark blood. Great white shark flesh. I didn't know whether to laugh or shout, both difficult to do with a regulator gripped in one's mouth. Where to sequester safely this singular trophy? Bending, I unzipped one bootie and slid the tooth inside, then zipped the neoprene back up. I could feel the tooth pressing against my ankle, hard and unyielding and still sharp.

Outside, several hundred similar teeth are cruising back and forth, still in firm possession of their owners. Mine will not be missed. I resumed shooting.

Back on board, my fellow divers expressed envy and delight at the sight of the tooth. It looked smaller on the boat and in the daylight, but what it represented to me grew greater by the minute.

Later, when I removed my wet suit, I was in so much pain I couldn't climb into my bunk. I had to lever myself in. Turning over was agony. For the remainder of the expedition, I didn't sleep well, nor was I able to return to the water for another dive.

No matter. I'd had my half hour alone with the masters of the earth's oceans. I would be returning home with my memories and with video—and with the tooth.

I also returned with a hairline fracture of one or more ribs, but somehow that didn't matter, either.

III

FELIX

Mount Etjo, Namibia, November 1993

ARIZONA HAS BEEN MY HOME for a third of a century. It's a visually arresting corner of the world—towering flat-topped buttes, winding canyons of multihued candy-striped stone, rivers that sink out of sight and turn to sand in the dry season, hardy vegetation that half the time is unable to decide if it's cactus or not, indomitable animals and insects that manage to eke out a rugged existence in a tough, unforgiving, highly variable climate, and birds that, of necessity, seem to possess vision just a little sharper than that of close relatives that have an easier time of life elsewhere.

It looks just like Namibia.

But while the vegetation in Namibia is no less confused than its North American relatives and the birds that patrol its startlingly unpolluted sky have sight equally acute, the animals and insects are very different. As a general rule, the insects of Southwest Africa, whose barren and melancholy shores Namibia fronts, are relatively harmless. For one thing, they're too busy trying to collect enough moisture to stay alive to spend time producing poisons. But the animals—ah, the animals . . .

You know you're not in Arizona when a pack of baboons runs across the highway in front of your car.

Yes, Arizona has its predators. Foremost is the cougar, or mountain lion, star of many a Hollywood film and hysterical news report as well as innumerable nature documentaries. Then there is its smaller cousin, the bobcat. The Mexican wolf has been reintroduced in Arizona, with sporadic success. If infrequent rare sightings are to be believed, the occasional solemn and ghostly jaguar also intermittently crosses the border from Mexico to hunt, mate, and scout ancient traditional territories from which single-minded ranchers expelled it a hundred years ago. There are also foxes and, most notably, the ubiquitous coyote. Contrary to its enduring and endearing cartoon adventures, the coyote is far too smart to engage in futile pursuit of lightening-quick roadrunners when the countryside is full of plump rabbits, nut-stuffed ground squirrels, and more frequently these days, clueless suburbanite mini-mutts.

But from there the larger mammalian population of Namibia diverges sharply from its Arizona relations. Perhaps it's just as well. One wonders at the psychic shock a pack of American coyotes would suffer were they suddenly to be confronted by a foraging elephant.

Far from the overdeveloped, overpopulated centers of civilization in the Northern Hemisphere, Namibia still boasts healthy numbers of leopards, lions, jackals, hyenas, and numerous smaller carnivores. For many people, the most admirable member of the Namibian pantheon of predators is that fastest and most gracile of all the big cats: the cheetah (*Acinonyx jubatus*). Sleek of line, limber of build, with a strikingly marked face that is more doglike than that of any other feline, the patient cheetah was a favored pet of ancient Egyptian nobility. Or so the legends say.

It's difficult for those of us who are non-royalty to envision successfully keeping a big cat as a pet. At one time or another, my wife and I have shared our home with half a dozen house cats that lumped together wouldn't weigh as much as a healthy cheetah's full belly. The outrageous thought of having one of the pharaoh's favorites freely roaming the kitchen and the rest of the house was a notion destined to remain forever a fragment of little more than dreams and fantasy.

Until I met Felix.

I had not been in Namibia very long, and I can't remember who it was who recommended that on my way north to the Etosha National Park I should stop and pay a visit to the Mount Etjo Safari Lodge, but a glance at the map showed that it was not terribly far off the main highway. And at 150 miles from the capital, Windhoek, it would make a nice break in the journey to the famed wildlife reserve. Unsure of the driving time, the condition of the highway, or much else in this strange new land that looked exactly like my home state, I figured I could easily give the place a pass if I found myself running short on time.

My informant told me that the turn-off was well marked. And so it was. A few hours out of Windhoek and already in the middle of nowhere, I came upon a large sign indicating that the lodge lay about twenty-five miles almost due west of where I was parked. Standing outside my vehicle flanked by mountains, high veldt, and little else, I took stock of my surroundings. Even here, on the side of the most important road in the country, there was virtually no traffic. This is understandable once one realizes that for Namibia the highway connection southward to South Africa is of far more significance than any need to reach Angola by road.

I was tired, but not exhausted. Should I continue on to Otjiwarongo, or take my casual acquaintance's recommendation and detour west for a couple of days? Slipping back into my rented Toyota, I turned left and started down the well-maintained dirt road.

The lodge at Mount Etjo (where on March 21, 1990, the Namibian Declaration of Independence had been signed) was even nicer than advertised. Though the weather was incredibly hot, I immediately signed up to stay over for a couple of nights and agreed to join the next available game drive. Situated amid the Okonjati Wildlife Sanctuary's 75,000 acres of wilderness, the lodge offered plenty to see, from kudu and Damara dik-diks to hippos and friendly elephants—including one young female that insistently kept trying to purloin an Italian visitor's camera.

Hot, sweaty, and tired after the game drive, the other four travelers hurried from the 4x4 to their cool rooms. Hot, sweaty, and energized, I decided to take a walk. Like sex, the prospect of a freshwater shower in a sizzling climate is enhanced the longer it is delayed.

It was while wandering around the lodge compound that I came upon an enclosure demarcated by a flimsy wall of chicken wire. No more than five feet high at any point, it seemed wholly inadequate to contain anything bigger than a languorous desert tortoise. Wiping sweat from my eyes with the back of my hand, I decided that it was empty. Searching the interior, I noted a few scrubby plants, sand, and some scraggly shade trees. Nothing else but shadows.

Then one of the shadows moved.

My eyes widened, and my heart beat a little faster. Off to my left and right beside the insubstantial fence, something sleek and powerful was stirring in the shady indistinctness of a dappled patch of soil. I took a couple of steps toward it. It moved again. Then it yawned. I had a glimpse of teeth, fur, legs. Leopard? No, surely not. Not in that pen, whose fragile barrier any healthy child could easily have pushed over.

A voice startled me. So focused was I on the softly panting shape of the full-grown male cheetah that I hadn't heard the guide come up behind me.

"That's Felix." The man with the strong South African accent nodded in the big cat's direction. The afternoon heat was oppressive, slowing my thoughts as well as my movements. "Would you like to meet him?"

"Uh, meet him?"

The guide smiled. "It's up to you. If you're willing to go inside his enclosure, I'll take you in. You can interact."

Interact. Under the circumstances, it was a word pregnant with more than one possible outcome. I looked once more at the wobbly fence. Describing it as frail would have flattered it.

"Can't he get out?"

"Oh, sure," the guide said. "But he doesn't. It's his home." He proceeded to tell me the cheetah's story.

Felix's mother had been killed by a car or truck. Of her two cubs, found alone and crying by the roadside, only Felix was still alive. His sibling had been killed by a mamba. Now Felix was fully mature, and this cockleshell compound was his home. If he really wanted to, he could likely leave any time he so desired, even though, unlike many cats, cheetahs are poor climbers. I looked again at the barrier. It would not have to be climbed. A single leap would allow its sole occupant to clear it.

Torn between desire and common sense, I debated. "Are you sure this is OK?" Wearing proper safari clothes didn't make me a shikari.

The guide shrugged. "Felix knows me. You should be OK as long as I'm with you."

Should be. Since childhood it had been a dream of mine to get close to one of the big cats. I think it must be a dream everyone has. If such an encounter came to pass, I had always imagined it would take place at some shopping-mall Christmastime photo-op and involve a well-fed veteran feline performer from the movies or television, or perhaps at a private zoo featuring an elderly people-habituated lion used to having its picture taken alongside giggling children clutching its scruffy mane. Not in the middle of northern Namibia amid heat and sand and far greater variables. I told myself that having been raised by humans, Felix might qualify as half-domesticated.

Of course, that also meant he qualified as half-wild.

I had not come to Namibia on a wine-tasting tour. I nodded at the guide. "Let's go in."

Maybe it was only a chicken-wire fence, but once I was standing *inside* the enclosure, the meager meandering barrier suddenly seemed a lot more substantial than it had from the other side. The guide picked up a well-chewed hard rubber sphere about the size of a volleyball and tossed it.

"Here, Felix! Get your toy, Felix. Go get it."

At the sound of the encouraging guide's voice, the cheetah lifted his head, looked at the man a moment, and then slumped back down. The guide continued to try to get Felix to play, or just to stand up. Just as studiously, the cheetah ignored him. Standing nearby and watching, I was acutely conscious of still being encased in a veneer of gummy sweat and dust from the afternoon game drive. *Shower*, I thought longingly. But instead of leaving, I made myself stand there and study the recumbent, somnolent carnivore. Heat be damned: I knew these were precious moments not to be wasted.

Felix was big, full-grown, but compared to a lion or tiger not at all that intimidating. *Acinonyx jubatus* resides in its own genus. Famed as the fastest of all land animals, capable of reaching speeds of nearly eighty miles an hour, the cheetah can accelerate from a standing start to seventy miles per hour in three seconds. A Porsche can't do that. Neither can a Ferrari.

Felix, it was becoming increasingly apparent, was disinclined to provide proof.

The guide kept tossing the ball. With great dignity, Felix continued to ignore both it and him. While it was a privilege simply to be permitted to stand in such close unbarred proximity to such a magnificent animal, the afternoon heat was making me drowsy. Surely, now it was time to leave and partake of the refreshing delights of my room. Or to do something else. Anything to alleviate the tedium and the heat.

Instead of backing toward the exit, I heard myself saying, "Can I get closer to him?"

The guide shrugged. Was that a smile filled with humor, or a cautioning one? "Up to you."

It seemed as if everything and anything was up to me. Handing the guide my video camera and asking him to shoot some footage, I walked slowly over to Felix, never taking my eyes off him. My deliberate and careful approach aroused him not at all. He didn't so much as twitch. Slowly, I crouched down beside him. From what seemed like a great distance, I heard the guide say, "He likes to be petted and scratched on his head."

O-o-o-o-h . . . k-a-a-a-y. Reaching out with my right hand, I began to stroke the fur between the cheetah's ears, exercising a firm, consistent motion. *After all*, I kept telling myself, *you have six cats at home, and this is just another cat.* Each time I slid my fingers forward onto his forehead, I was acutely conscious of how close they were to that closed mouth.

Without looking in my direction, Felix lifted his head slightly and began to purr.

I had no idea what to expect from the encounter, but I did not anticipate that. It was a perfectly normal, ordinary, familiar feline purr. Deeper than that emitted by our cats at home, but unmistakable. It was one of the most beautiful sounds I have ever heard in my life. I am sure the uncontainable smile that spread across my face made me look like a prime candidate for the post of village idiot, but I didn't care.

I stayed like that, petting and stroking Felix, until the guide began to fidget. Unnoticed by me, half an hour had passed in the late afternoon heat.

"Had enough?" he finally asked me.

Utterly and completely subsumed in the magic of the moment, I would have stayed until my thighs gave out and I toppled over, but his query reminded me of the time and the temperature. "Almost," I replied. Our cats enjoyed being scratched between their front legs. At least half full of confidence now, I reached forward and began to scratch Felix on his chest, between his lanky but muscular front legs.

Something *whizzed* past my face. I felt the slightest brush of wind. It happened so quickly that only after the fact did I realize what had taken place. At the same time, I became aware that Felix had twisted his upper body around, turned his head, opened his mouth, and was looking straight at me. He was holding his right leg up, the paw pointed at my face. For the first time, I could see his teeth clearly. The killing canines were much, much bigger than I would have imagined.

The guide had immediately lowered the video camera. His voice had tensed slightly. "That's interesting," he said evenly. "I didn't know he didn't like that."

You didn't know . . . ? You didn't *know*?

I know I flinched. But in a crouching position, with my thighs and calves already thoroughly cramped from maintaining the same posture for so long, I couldn't do more than flinch without falling down. That would have put me flat on the ground, which I suspected would have been A Really Bad Idea. I stared at Felix. Felix stared at me. Then he lowered his foreleg and resumed facing forward. And did something that in its own way was even more shocking than the warning swipe he had taken at my face.

He meowed.

I swear, it was a cartoon dialogue-balloon meow. A perfect Sylvester-the-Cat meow. I knew cheetahs might purr. I knew they barked. But *meow*? The guide had shut off the video camera as soon as the cat had swung at me, so we missed recording the sound. Mentally, I tried to reconcile what I had just experienced with what I had just heard. Was the cat apologizing? Laughing? Teasing?

First I'll rip your face off, then—meow.

Reviewing the video later, I was able to see what my eyes had not been able to register when the incident had occurred. Felix's semi-retractable claws (semi-retractable claws are known only in three other cat species) had missed my nose by about an inch. The cheetah had known exactly what he had been doing.

Don't scratch my chest.

I counted myself fortunate. Very fortunate indeed. Had Felix been in a more irritable mood, he could just as easily have taken my nose off. Or bit down on the offending hand. Instead, he had chosen only to warn me. Maybe it was the heat. Maybe at night, or on a cooler afternoon, it might have gone differently.

Handing my camera back to me, the guide said casually, "You mentioned earlier than your wife is an ex–vet tech, and that you have some land in Arizona with a horse stable and a high fence."

"Thirteen acres." I wiped sweat from my forehead. My eyes were burning. "Why?"

That half smile again. "We have more animals than we can take care of here. Would you be interested in taking Felix home with you? We could prepare the necessary export papers, handle quarantine arrangements, and so on."

He's putting me on, I thought. *Probably plays the same gag on everyone who spends time with the cat.*

But what if it *wasn't* a joke . . .

I gave the offer serious thought. Really serious thought. For about thirty seconds. Not because I didn't think I could get along with Felix. Not because our thirteen acres of terrain virtually identical to what he was familiar with here at Mount Etjo would be unsuitable for him. Not because I worried that he might scare our own cats inside out. But because I don't believe in keeping big cats, or any big animal with the exception of a horse or a llama, as a pet.

I've been torn up pretty good by the claws of house cats. They can bite, too. Dogs also bite. So do babies. My philosophy on keeping big cats as pets is twofold.

First, it's a silly and unnecessary paradigm of macho self-aggrandizement.

Second, you can keep a big cat as a pet for years. You can sleep with it, eat with it, play with it, swim with it, let your family nuzzle it while they're watching TV. And then the cat has one bad hair day. If it's a house cat, you get a scratch. If it's a dog, you get a nip. If it's a kid, you get yelled at and maybe cussed out.

If it's a big cat, you lose something else. Like maybe the kid. So I put the idea out of my head permanently, if not instantly.

Those thirty seconds of serious consideration lingered in my mind for an unusually long time.

Before I left the compound, Felix stood up and stretched. I can tell you that a full-grown male cheetah standing up is a helluva lot more striking than one that is lying down. The attenuated body and the impressively long legs make for one deceptively large animal. Had Felix chosen to stand on his hind legs and put his forelegs on my shoulders, he could easily have looked me in the eye. But we had already done that last bit.

So there you have it. A fragment of knowledge you won't find in the guidebooks and one I inadvertently added to the local lore at Mount Etjo. The next male cheetah you meet, don't try to scratch him between his front legs.

Not even for the chance of hearing him meow.

IV

THE CUTE LITTLE OCTOPUS AND THE HOMICIDAL SHELL

East Central Australia, November 1989

MY WIFE AND I WERE standing on the sweltering tarmac at the little airport in Bundaberg, Queensland, Australia, waiting beside our modest luggage to depart for Lady Elliot Island. I had heard a great deal about the unspoiled beauty of isolated Lady Elliot, usually promoted as the southernmost island on the Great Barrier Reef, and we were both looking forward to a few days' respite from our planned long drive up the coast from Brisbane to still-distant Cape Tribulation.

Assuming the well-used aircraft parked in front of us could get us there in one piece, of course.

I don't like flying. I've had some stunning flights in tiny planes and ghastly flights in big planes and vice versa, but the discomfort and unease in my gut never goes away. The veteran Twin Otter parked before us was already crammed to the gills with supplies for the island's solitary resort. As the only passengers on this particular flight, we were allowed to seat ourselves wherever we could find space among the stacked crates of biscuits, boxes of canned goods, and cartons of bottled drinks, many of the latter from Bundaberg's own excellent local brewery.

"Where's the rest of the plane?" my wife asked as we prepared to board.

Fortunately, the air was calm and clear, and the flight itself thankfully devoid of literal ups and downs. Landing on Lady Elliot presented an interesting prospect of its own. There is something unsettling about small island airstrips that extend all the way from one side of your destination to the other. Come in too short, and you end up in the water. Delay touchdown too long or fail to brake in time, and you end up in the water.

I've always been grateful that my love of being in the water tends to cancel out my fear of flying over it.

We and our minimal baggage were soon settled in our comfortable if basic room, luxuriating in the island's much-advertised tranquillity, the flitting about of hyperactive sparrow-size yellow-tinged silvereyes twittering in the pisonia trees, and the rhythmic flush of wavelets breaking on the nearby shore. Lady Elliot is not an atoll, but an island with a fringing reef, so at high tide the water rolls all the way in to the island.

While JoAnn rested, I did an afternoon dive with a small group of fellow visitors and one of the more unpleasant dive masters I've ever encountered, but I enjoyed myself anyway. I always do in the water. Whenever I'm diving I'm reminded of Peter O'Toole's statement while portraying Lawrence of Arabia in the film of the same name. When asked what it is that he, Lawrence, finds so appealing about the desert, O'Toole flatly replies, "It's clean." In the context of O'Toole's cinematic characterization of Lawrence, this brief response holds many meanings. I think of it often when I'm diving.

When the tide is out at Lady Elliot, visitors are permitted to walk on and to explore the shallow fringing reef. As my wife doesn't dive, this offered her the chance to observe at close range those sea creatures caught in pools left by the receding waters as well as those who dwell permanently in the intertidal zone. Reef walking is something anyone can do, but it's not as casual or danger-free an exercise as it is often portrayed in tourist advertisements.

To begin with, you need to have appropriate footwear. Simple sandals, flip-flops, and cheap open shoes just won't do. Coral can cut like a knife. Your feet need more than a minimal amount of protection. Ragged coral can also slice and dice footgear that is insufficiently durable. One of the quickest routes I know to a hospital is to be caught hiking far out on a reef with inadequate footwear. Coral not only cuts, it infects, and coral infections can be damnably difficult to cure and reluctant to heal.

Your feet can slip out of cheap sandals. Coral constitutes a rough walking surface whose unevenness is further disguised by the action and visual distortions caused by rippling water. Your favorite footwear may be tough, but if it doesn't provide proper support for your feet and ankles, you're better off skipping a reef walk, however enticing it seems. Nothing can bring a vacation to a miserable, screeching halt faster than a twisted knee or broken leg.

The best shoes I've found for reef walking are the booties scuba divers don before slipping on their fins. Booties are tough, designed to be submerged in salt water all the time, and many styles are equipped with ribbed soles suitable for limited hiking. They come with an added benefit in that they can be used with fins, even if all you do is snorkel. Compared to booties, expensive reef-walker shoes, Tevas and their clones, and plastic sandals don't hold up. If you don't have booties, I suggest bringing along a pair of expendable sneakers.

Because it's not only the inanimate sharp-edged coral that you have to look out for.

Reefs and their inhabitants are among the most amazing places on the planet. But like every other ecologically rich biota, they are home to hunters as well as the hunted, and sometimes the hunters are less than obvious.

When discussing diving I'm often asked, "Aren't you afraid of the sharks?" Let me tell you—whether on land or in the water, it's not the big predators you have to worry about. It's the little guys. The chance of being attacked by a shark, or a lion, or a bear, is far smaller than that of contracting a tropical disease, or acquiring an inimical internal parasite, or a persistent infection. It's smaller than that of meeting up with one of Nature's miniaturized but no less deadly predators. As any Australian who has been stung by an irukandji jellyfish (and survived) can tell you.

Cephalopods are all carnivores. Their class is comprised of squid, octopus, cuttlefish, and that living fossil, the chambered nautilus. They are the most intelligent of all invertebrates. Unlike a fish, when you confront a cephalopod, especially a cuttlefish or octopus, and gaze into its remarkably advanced eyes, you get the distinct feeling that something is looking back at you and . . . thinking. Their parrotlike beaks are powerful enough to crush the shells of mollusks to get at the edible flesh within. When biting, some species drip toxins of varying potency into the wound they inflict in order to help immobilize their prey. Sadly, they only live two or three years. I've always wondered how our species would have fared if intelligent cephalopods enjoyed life spans akin to that of humans. Perhaps one day genetic engineering would allow . . .

"Come look at the pretty octopus!"

I was preoccupied with examining some small fish isolated in a tidal pool when JoAnn called out to me. At her shout, I immediately left the fish to their sanctuary and carefully made my way over to my wife. Kneeling in shallow water that occasionally lapped over her ankles, she was poking and prodding at something just beneath the surface. I couldn't see what it was until I drew much closer.

When I saw what it was she was toying with, I'm sure my heart skipped a beat.

"Stop that," I said. I think I was too taken aback to speak loudly. "Stand up and step back."

She looked up at me. "Why? Isn't it pretty?"

"Please, hon. Just step back."

As a point of pride as well as amusement, JoAnn will usually argue anything with me, grinning as she does so. There must have been something in my voice, because she looked at me uncertainly and then, thankfully, stood up and took a step backward. She was wearing tough but open-toed sandals. Grateful for my ankle-high diving booties, I advanced gingerly and leaned over to get a better look at what she had been casually fingering. If I had guessed wrong as to its identity, I would be forced to own up to my ignorance. A cloud momentarily slid in front of the equatorial sun, fortuitously eliminating most of the glare coming off the gently rippling water.

I hadn't been wrong. As an ex–veterinary technician, my wife knows animals, their habits, and how to handle them. She knows the wild creatures of Texas and Arizona particularly well. But the only places in Texas and Arizona where you're likely to encounter meandering cephalopods are the cool depths of public aquariums.

Irritated by the attention and exposed by the receding tide, the octopus working its way over and through the miniature coraline canyons was smaller than my closed fist. I knew it was annoyed by all the interest it had attracted because of the bright, black-lined, almost iridescent blue rings it was presently flaring all over its tiny body.

My abrupt concern for my wife was due to the fact that this was a blue-ringed octopus; a species with a seriously poisonous bite. How poisonous? The venom in its defensive saliva (the octopus manufactures two kinds of venom: one to use in predation and the other for defense) contains tetrodotoxin, 5-hydroxytryptamine, hyaluronidase, tyramine, histamine, tryptamine, octopamine, taurine, acetylcholine, and dopamine: a litany of poisons sufficient to frighten even a non-chemist.

Tetrodotoxin in particular is a killer. Once this sodium blocker is injected into the body, it causes neuromuscular paralysis and sometimes full respiratory stoppage, often resulting in cardiac arrest and death. Since the victim is unable to breathe, the only chance of saving someone who has been bitten is to immediately initiate mouth-to-mouth respiration and continue it until the victim can be put on an artificial respirator. This treatment has to begin before the victim develops cyanosis and hypotension. Meanwhile, the poisoned individual can lie paralyzed but perfectly aware of everything that is taking place around them, unable to speak, breathe on their own, or indicate any symptoms of distress. It's a virtual living death.

Suddenly, the brightly hued little octopus doesn't seem so adorable anymore.

I explained all this in equally graphic but less biochemically heavy terms as we stood together, looking on from a short but safe distance away as the aggravated cephalopod continued to wriggle its way through the holes and rifts in the coral. Gradually, it calmed down, losing its warning blue rings in the process. JoAnn turned to me.

"You're not putting me on, are you?"

I shook my head slowly. "You were playing with it. *Touching* it. It could have killed you at any time."

She pondered. I've watched my wife skin a rattlesnake with her bare hands. There's not much she's afraid of. "Would have been a short vacation."

I nodded. Sometimes it's not only bold, but sensible, to be afraid.

There was nothing more to say. The sun was starting to set. Silently, we turned and began the long, careful hike that would take us across the reef and back to shore.

* * *

Speaking of tetrodotoxin . . .

Years later, I found myself diving in Papua New Guinea off the stern of a wonderful dedicated live-aboard dive boat called the *Tiata*. We were in warm, sunlit waters off the island of New Ireland, in the northern Bismarck Sea. It was an easy dive: little current, a sandy bottom, vast schools of rainbow-tinted anthias and butterfly fish, close to shore. What divers like to call an aquarium dive. No sharks to speak of, no sea snakes, nothing likely to cause trouble or pose a threat.

But remember, it's the little things that get you.

The gracious, middle-aged woman diving off to my right was from Chicago. In the course of the preceding days, she had revealed herself to be a competent diver, if not a terribly experienced one. Her husband, unfortunately, was the worst diver with whom I had ever been forced to share boat space. Armed with thousands of dollars' worth of camera equipment he had little idea how to use, he had absolutely no regard for his fellow divers, his dazzling but easily damaged natural surroundings, his inordinately patient spouse, or, insofar as I could tell, anything else save his own selfish interests. He had from the first day on board proven himself to be as self-centered and inconsiderate underwater as he was above it.

One day, having failed to get the underwater footage he sought and, as usual, entirely absorbed in himself, he literally shoved aside my cabinmate in his grumbling haste to get a cup of java from the boat's always-on coffeepot. I had to all but physically restrain my genial cabinmate, an ex–police forensics specialist from Australia, from bodily picking up the oblivious and obnoxious Chicagoan and heaving him overboard. The rest of us did our best to ignore our disagreeable fellow passenger while commiserating silently with his incredibly tolerant wife.

The next morning, the insufferable schmuck was off somewhere hanging onto live coral and shoving his camera in the faces of helpless fish in his usual futile attempt to get good pictures so he could boast to acquaintances back home about what a great photographer he was when I noticed his long-suffering spouse collecting shells from the channel's sandy bottom.

Shell collecting is a harmless enough activity when engaged in on land. Underwater, where the shells frequently still boast their original occupants, it can be quite a different matter. The marine gastropod mollusks that occupy most shells tend to be harmless—but not all of them. I wasn't watching over her—her husband was her nominal dive partner, and I was far more interested in inspecting the surrounding soft corals for tiny squat lobsters and harlequin shrimp—but by sheer chance I did happen to notice when she reached down for one particular shell. It was a large cone shell, saturated with color and the repeating geometric motifs for which its kind are known.

Certain cone shells are also known for something considerably less aesthetically pleasing.

When people think of harpoons, their thoughts automatically gravitate toward whaling and its dramatic, bloody history. They are not inclined to think of pretty shells. As is so often the case with Nature, this is another oversight, because cone shells are natural harpooners. Actually, what they "fire," by means of a sharp muscular contraction,

ALAN DEAN FOSTER

is a modified radular tooth (properly called a toxoglosson radula) that
contains a powerful neurotoxin. In some species, this is a tetrodotoxin.
That's right. Though they look nothing alike, some cone shells and
the blue-ringed octopus make use of the same ferocious type of poison.
And just like the venom of the blue-ringed octopus, there is no known
antidote or antivenom for the toxin of the cone shell.

I think there are instances when I have covered more space underwater in less time, but not many. I got to the woman before her bare fingers
could close around the shell. She looked at me in surprise when I grabbed
her wrist and pulled her hand away. Some concepts are easy to convey
underwater, others less so. I couldn't draw a finger across my throat to
indicate my concern because underwater that's the signal for someone
who is out of air. So I had to settle for shaking my finger at her confused
face, pointing down at the shell, grabbing my throat with both hands,
closing my eyes, and arching backward to drift limply in the water. That
particular pantomime sequence is not in any diver's manual, but it got the
point across. She looked at the shell, then back at me, and nodded, eyes
wide behind her mask.

Back on the boat, I took the time to enlighten her as to what had
inspired the brief but serious melodrama.

"It was so pretty," she murmured, "and it looked harmless."

I nodded. "Sure. That's what makes it so dangerous. A lionfish *looks*
dangerous, so nobody tries to grab it. Same with a spiny sea urchin. In
contrast, a shell is just—a shell. Except when it's a live cone shell."

She nodded back at me. "Maybe I'll just stick to collecting shells on
the beach."

"Good idea. And while we're on the subject . . ."

"Yes?"

"Just in case the occasion should present itself, you should avoid trying to shake hands with any pretty little octopuses, too."

V

JEALOUS ANTS, MILLIONS OF ANTS, AND REALLY, REALLY BIG...ANTS

Southeastern Peru, May 1987

THERE MAY BE NO OTHER place in the world as magnificently wild and biologically diverse as Manú National Park in southeastern Peru. At 3.7 million acres, approximately the size of the state of New Jersey, Manú encompasses within its boundaries 13,000-foot Andean heights, spectacular untouched cloud forest, and glorious unspoiled lowland Amazonian rain forest. More than 15,000 kinds of plants have been found in Manú, more than 625 varieties of tree can inhabit a single acre, and the park is home to more than 800 species of birds, almost as many as in all of North America.

Only a small part of this extraordinary example of still intact Amazonia is open to the public. Another somewhat larger section, mostly along the Alto Madre de Dios River, has been made available by the Peruvian government for mixed use. The great majority of the park is maintained in its original, natural, untouched state and is open only to scientists and government-approved explorers. Within its boundaries can be found perambulating spectacled bears, the raucous cock-of-the-rock (Peru's national bird), innumerable snakes, macaws, parrots, primates, giant otters, giant catfish, rare black caimans, piranhas of varying size, species, and disposition, towering trees, entangling vines, the dreaded candiru, at least two human tribes that have essentially no contact with the outside world, and potentially thousands upon thousands of undiscovered, unnamed, and unstudied creatures of every order and genus.

There are also an awful lot of ants.

I first visited Manú in 1987, the year it was declared a World Heritage Site by UNESCO. At that time, there was no place close to the park's boundaries where interested visitors could stay, and certainly nowhere within them. Besides the single primitive ranger station precariously situated at the edge of the Manú River near the entrance to the park, a single scientific station was located much deeper inside the park boundaries on the shores of Cocha Cashu, a small oxbow lake. Quite properly, this facility was and still is closed to non-researchers. In charge of its supervision was the eminent ecologist John Terborgh, whose book *Requiem for Nature*, set largely in Manú, I highly recommend.

Asking around the modern Andean city and ancient Inca capital of Cusco (or Cuzco, or if you want to really be a stickler, Qosqo in Quechua) about the possibility of visiting Manú, my traveling companion Mark and I were told to try and find a certain Boris Gómez Luna, as he was the only one who could conceivably arrange such a visit on short notice. Though his name made him sound like a character from a John Le Carré novel, Boris turned out to be a slight, charming fellow whose unexpected youth was matched only by his dedication to and enthusiasm for the wild Manú. Though in the years that have passed Boris has since moved on to bigger things, his enthusiasm for Manú has never flagged.

Señor Gómez Luna, we learned, was in the process of building the first facility inside the park that would be permitted to accommodate non-researchers. In other words, visitors like Mark and myself. Could we possibly, we inquired when we finally managed to track him down, make some arrangement with him to spend a week or so in Manú?

"I can organize it for you," he told us in his excellent English, "but nothing is finished there. We're still in the beginning stages of construction, and you'll have to sleep in a tent like the rest of the construction crew, eat the same food, utilize the same facilities. And you can't bring much with you. I need the space in the truck for supplies." We immediately and eagerly accepted, and a price was agreed upon.

Two days later, we were picked up by Boris in his hulking, specially reinforced Nissan Patrol 4x4 and struggled to squeeze ourselves and our backpacks in among the mountain of materials and equipment he had collected for the journey. The road out of Cusco soon turned from pavement to dirt and began to wind its way through high treeless mountain canyons horizontally striped with perfectly level ancient Inca stone terraces. Vistas turned grand and wide. Like mice in a nest, simple houses clustered together at the bottom of increasingly deep river valleys. Irregularly shaped irrigated fields and neat square plots linked the vast expanses of bare rock together like bright green patches on a heavily weathered gray overcoat.

Many hours later, we reached the high pass near the turnoff to Tres Cruces and came to a stop. Though the view over the clouds and mountains to the east was as spectacular as it was sobering, I found myself wondering about the delay. Boris proceeded to explain.

"From here all the way down to the Upper Madre de Dios, the road is one way. From noon to midnight, traffic is allowed to go down. From midnight to noon, traffic can come up." He checked his watch. "We must wait a few more minutes."

Hacked, hoed, and blasted out of winding, cloud-forest-swathed, perpetually damp and foggy mountainsides, the road from the Tres Cruces turnoff down to the backcountry Amazonian town of Pilcopata offered one of the two most hair-raising drives I have ever experienced (the other was also in Peru, from Chachapoyas to the citadel of Kuelap). Everyone is afraid of something. Sharks, bees, spiders, the dark, enclosed spaces: Me, I don't like heights. So I was thankful for the thick clouds and mist that blotted out the view below us.

Hours later and only partway to our destination, we encountered a characteristically overloaded truck illegally making its way upward. The Patrol halted, sliding slightly on the muddy track. It had been in four-wheel-drive mode ever since we had commenced our descent.

"You might want to get out of the car and watch," a thoughtful Boris advised us. Mark and I hastily complied, beating a judicious retreat up the rain-swept road. Standing there in slick, shallow mud with a light drizzle falling, we watched open-mouthed as our genial and unflappable host and the tight-lipped truck driver embarked upon an agonizingly slow, incredibly patient, and exceedingly dangerous vehicular pas de deux. While the clumsy, top-heavy truck scraped and hugged the fern-encrusted rock wall, Boris gingerly edged the Patrol around it. At one point, the 4x4's rear right wheel was literally hanging over a sheer drop with nothing beneath it save hundreds of feet of fog. Eyes wide, we held our breath until the wheel once more caught solid ground and dug in, and the pass-by was complete.

Wiping mist from my forehead and face as I clambered back into the Patrol, I was unashamedly unstinting in my praise of Boris's driving. Having just casually cheated death and disaster, he shrugged off our compliments.

"I have to do it all the time. Nobody pays much attention to the guidelines."

Mark leaned forward from where he was crammed, pretzellike, among the jumble of supplies. "Uh, anybody ever go over the edge?"

Boris's voice didn't change. He was concentrating on the mist-shrouded single-lane road ahead. "Oh, sure. All the time. When it's a bus, it can be really bad."

I looked out the window. It was starting to get dark, and I was glad of it. Now I wouldn't have to contemplate the fog, or the nothingness that it masked. I envisioned dozens of decrepit, twisted, rusting buses lying in the deep ravine below the road like the carcasses of so many dead dinosaurs.

We spent the night at a plantation on the other side of the Alto Madre de Dios enjoying the comfort of real beds. Waking us were the raucous shouts of macaws, parrots, and, in particular, the greater and lesser oro-pendula, whose melodious bell-like calls sounded like a chorus of flautists tuning up to play Debussy or Ravel. Leaving immediately after a break-fast whose white veranda setting was straight out of Somerset Maugham, we started downriver. In the heavily loaded, attenuated, motorized dugout, the journey took longer than anticipated. It did not occur to me until much later that the weight of two extra bodies in the supply canoe might have played havoc with Boris's calculations and accustomed schedule. If such was the case, he very diplomatically never said a word about it.

Powering up the Manú River after a brief stop at the wannabe town of Boca Manú, we soon began to encounter enormous logjams comprised of huge trees that had been swept down the river by the annual rainy season floods. The irresistible power of water was evident all around us. As we maneuvered to go around one such pile, movement on its crest caught my eye.

Standing at the apex of a two-story-high jumble of gigantic mahogany logs stood a huge Matsigenka. Naked save for a pair of donated and incongruously colorful shorts, he was holding a portable chainsaw in one hand and waving cheerfully to us with the other as we motored past. One of Boris's employees, he was engaged in cutting wood for the lodge-to-be. I will forever remember him standing there, a shirtless black-haired warrior content to do solitary battle with immense tree trunks that had been thrown together like the pieces from a giant's game of pickup sticks.

The sun falls fast in the tropics. Though forced to slow our speed because of the darkness, we continued upriver. Standing in the bow, Boris trained a spotlight the size of a half-gallon jug on the water ahead. From time to time, he would call out instructions to the boatman manning the tiller. A pair of eyes like gold coins flashed on the starboard riverbank, and our host quickly swung his light around. Caught momentarily in its glare, something small, swift, and spotted snarled softly at us before whirling to vanish into the jungle.

"Jaguarundi," Boris informed us. "Not easy to see."

There was nothing to indicate the turnoff for the lodge site: no sign, no mark on the seasonally shifting riverbank. But both Boris and the boatman knew exactly where to pull in. While the men who had been waiting for the dugout began to unload the small mountain of supplies, our young host plunged into the dark jungle. Guided by flashlight and despite our fatigue buoyed up by excitement, we walked, slid, tripped, and stumbled through forest that closed in around us like a wet, clinging green blanket.

After an hour's walk, we emerged into a small clearing. In front of our exhausted eyes, an oxbow lake glistened magically in the moonlight: Cocha Salvador. The sharply defined silhouettes of tents stood out against the surrounding chaotic verdure. Directed to our individual peaked quarters, Mark and I collapsed on our respective sleeping bags. On, not in. The suffocating humidity rendered covering of any kind not only superfluous but intolerable.

Arising the following morning to the music of effervescent songbirds and the prehistoric caw of turkey-size hoatzins, we soon discovered that the bulk of Boris's time was taken up with supervising the construction of the lodge. Just as he had told us, it was still very much in the initial stages of construction. Proudly, he showed us where the visitors' rooms were going to go, the hygienic facilities, the meeting and dining center, the library. At present, every one of these was represented only by mahogany pillars that had been painstakingly driven into the reluctant ground.

"The whole complex is being built of salvaged mahogany." He grinned. "It may be the only all-mahogany lodge in the world. Ecologically sound, because all of the wood is salvage taken from the river. Also, mahogany is the only local wood white ants [termites] won't eat."

We had (I cannot say enjoyed) our meals in a large communal tent that I quickly dubbed *la casa de los mosquitos*, because there always seemed to be more mosquitoes humming around within than without. The mosquitoes of Manú have their own happy hour, during which time they leisurely sample whatever purported insect repellent you happen to have ineffectually slathered on your poor, defenseless body in the faint hope of dissuading them from pursuing their natural inclinations to act like a thousand diminutive Draculas. Having sipped their fill of your inadequate repellent and no doubt compared its vintage with that of previous years, they then turn their attention to the evening's main course: you. At such moments, I would grit my teeth and remind myself that the ferocious biting bugs of Manú are one reason the region remains relatively pristine and has not been overrun by prospectors and poachers.

Drenched in tepid perspiration day and night, we would have killed for a five-minute shower. As yet, the only showers at the site existed in Boris's plans for the lodge. But there was an alternative, if one was fast enough and brave enough and desperate enough to make use of it.

We were told that the diurnal mosquitoes of Manú clock out at precisely five-fifteen p.m. while their nocturnal counterparts don't report for work until five-thirty. This provided a fifteen-minute window—no more, no less—during which time every one of Boris's workers flung off their clothes like a clutch of Wall Street bankers suddenly converted to nudism, plunged madly into the lake, splashed about like a bunch of demented day-trippers from a Lima asylum, erupted from the water, and hastily reclothed themselves.

In the course of our first evening in Manú, Mark and I observed this frenzied and highly localized ritual with a mixture of amazement, envy, and trepidation. This was, after all, my first time in the Amazon and I was . . . leery.

"I guess there are no piranhas in the lake," I told Boris, who had chosen to forgo that evening's collective ablutions.

"Oh no," he corrected me cheerfully. "The *cocha* is full of piranhas. But they don't bother you unless the water level is very low or there is blood in the water. All that crazed stuff you see in the movies: That's just Hollywood. If you want, tomorrow we'll go fishing for piranhas. They're very good eating."

Uh-huh, I told myself. *And they no doubt think the reverse is true.* By day three, however, the accumulated caked sweat on my corpus was making me feel like an Egyptian mummy imprisoned in a California sauna, and the promise of cool water had grown too tempting to be ignored any longer. So it was that Mark and I found ourselves anxiously lined up facing the lakeshore along with Boris's milling mob of local indigenous and mestizo workers. Enjoying themselves immensely, they grinned at the two apprehensive gringos in their midst. I could understand but little of what they were saying, but their gestures were eloquent. Resolute but still uneasy, we smiled determinedly back.

The designated moment arrived. As if on command, the last biting insect vanished from the enveloping superheated air. And as though they had been vaporized, clothes slipped off swarthy, muscular bodies as twenty or so men of varying ethnic backgrounds and skin hues promptly plunged into the lake like so many naked schoolboys out of a bucolic Norman Rockwell painting. We all splashed about frantically, my friend and I in a delirium of delight as the almost chill water banished the accrued and all but crusted perspiration from our bodies.

Bathtime was up far too soon. Having been warned, we charged back to shore as fast as we had fled from it and hurriedly dressed ourselves—in the same sweat-soaked clothing from which we had just escaped. I felt like a moth forced to again take up residency in its icky, cast-off cocoon.

Twenty minutes later, we were again drenched in perspiration and glumly readying ourselves for another restless night's sleep.

One of the worst experiences I have ever gone through in my travels occurred the following night when the lower portion of my insides woke me from a fitful and restless slumber. Nocturnal urination was not a problem. It was performed outside one's tent, a few steps into the forest.

I did not have to urinate.

Fumbling through the darkness inside the tent, I found and checked my watch. My heart sank. It was a little after two-thirty in the morning. The living, breathing organism that was the Amazon was all around me. The sounds of the jungle at night are far more amenable when experienced in the comfort of one's own home as they emerge from a movie soundtrack or a pleasant mood–inducing recording. In the isolation and feverish reality of the sweltering rain forest itself, those same curious sounds can be, by turns, provoking or sinister. As an accompaniment to a suddenly overwhelming need to go to the bathroom at two-thirty in the morning in the middle of untouched jungle, their overall effect tends to incline toward the latter.

I remonstrated with my bowels. I told myself over and over that I didn't really have to go. I insisted to my intestines that they could wait until morning. With increasing urgency, my innards maintained otherwise. The brain disposes; the body imposes.

Crawling out of my tent, I flicked on my small flashlight. Its beam was distressingly short and narrow. Around me, the camp was completely silent. Locating the relevant trail that had been pointed out to us when we had first arrived, I began walking.

Few places on Earth are as dark as the rain forest at night. Like damp sheets, moist green-black walls close in around you on all sides. The forest's leaf-fingers reach out to touch you, to caress you, to explore you as you stride hurriedly forward, trying to have as little contact as possible with the crush of overripe life. It is not a place for claustrophobes.

At night in the jungle, a different flourish of life emerges to eat—and to hunt. Spiders as big as dinner plates, snakes whose venom can kill in minutes, giant scorpions and centipedes are joined by all manner of biting bugs gravid with parasites and infectious diseases, some of which are so rare or new they do not yet even have names, much less antidotes. Things that crawl and slither and jump are everywhere, and outside the thin civilizing beam of your flashlight, you cannot see a single one of them. Rustlings, movements, small flurries of sound from all sides tease and confuse your hearing and your sense of place.

Was that a movement? Quickly, you swing your light around, and you see nothing save perhaps the slight bobbing of a branch or the up-and-down quiver where a leaf has been disturbed. A subtle cough reaches you—perhaps a jaguar, lord of the rain forest? I walked faster.

The single pit toilet that had been dug to service the workers had necessarily been sited a good distance away from the lake and the camp. The smell of it was unavoidable, but oddly not overpowering. There was no roof over the small clearing, no walls surrounding it. A single rough bench seat was all that held the visitor safely clear of the suppurating ooze that lay below. Sitting there in the middle of the Amazonian night, nervously trying to dissect every crackle and peep and hoot while urging my convulsing digestive system to hurry and finish its work, I was not worried about what might be moving silently through the dark forest around me, or waiting to drop down from the tangle of branches above. All I could think of, all I could try not to imagine, was what might be lurking and slithering and slipping through the accumulated organic morass beneath my partially naked, vulnerable body. I would far rather face an angry armed man.

Ever since that night, in whatever corner of the planet I happen to find myself, I always make it a point before the sun sets to pay a visit to whatever sanitary facility is available—no matter how crude or seemingly unhygienic it may appear to be.

Another couple of days were to pass before I was to make the all-too intimate acquaintance of a singular ant.

Having found a little time to slip away from supervising construction of the lodge, Boris was guiding Mark and me on one of our longer hikes through the rain forest. As we walked, he enthusiastically pointed out colorful insects, named trees and bushes, and struggled to identify birds according to their songs and calls, careful always to give their scientific as well as common names. It was another steamy late afternoon. Tomorrow would also be hot and steamy, as would the day after that, and the day following. Unless it rained hard, in which case it would only be warm and damp for a while. Once the rain stopped, it would inevitably turn hotter and steamier than ever.

Quite unexpectedly, we came to a clearing in the forest.

It was immediately apparent that this was no inadvertent open space. A single tree stood in the middle of a parklike circle some twenty feet in diameter. The tree itself was not particularly impressive. The clearing that surrounded it was. The site looked as if it had just been mowed by some especially devoted golf course groundskeeper tending to a particularly loved piece of turf. Despite being surrounded on all sides by a rich, loamy, decaying mat of sodden and nourishing rain-forest detritus, not so much as a single green shoot poked its hopeful head skyward from the cleared area.

"*Palo santo.*" Boris pointed at the tree that was thriving in the center of the inexplicable circle. "The ants that live in the tree keep the area around it perfectly clear. Within the boundaries, nothing is allowed to live that might take nutrients or water from the tree or otherwise harm it. If something starts to grow, they cut it down. If it moves, they kill it or drive it away. In return, the tree gives the ants a home."

I had long read of such symbiotic ant-tree relationships. The fire ants that dwelled within the tangarana tree are called by the same name as their home: tangarana ants. They were not as widely known and did not have the same widespread malevolent cache as army ants or the dreaded isula ants, but they were feared nonetheless.

"Come, I'll show you." Boris started toward the solitary bole. Mark and I exchanged a glance and followed.

Up close, we studied the foot-thick tree trunk. There wasn't an ant in sight. Unsheathing his machete, Boris reversed it and using the solid haft began tapping lightly on the wood. Within seconds, the trunk was swarming with hundreds of ants. Observing them, I relaxed a little. Despite the frenetic activity they displayed as they searched for the source of the disturbance, they were no more than a quarter inch in length. I had already seen and photographed at close range much larger and far more threatening army ant soldiers. Taking out my video camera, I began recording the activity.

Having stepped back and resheathed his machete, Boris was watching me closely.

"Be careful. Don't let them get on you."

"I'm all right." Seen through the camera's viewfinder, the ants appeared oddly detached from reality, as if I was already viewing them in finished, edited form. I moved the camera lens closer, confident that I could get good pictures without making physical contact. After all, wasn't I already experienced at this? Why . . . I had already spent nearly a whole week in the Amazon rain forest.

An incredible searing pain shot through my left hand.

It seems that the enraged tangarana ants not only rush out to defend the trunk of their tree home—swarming into the branches, they fan out into the leaves to drop down onto any intruders below. I had been savagely attacked by a quarter-inch-long parachutist armed with a built-in hypodermic and a toxin that burned like fire.

Jumping back from the tree, I managed to hang on to the camera with my right hand while furiously shaking my left as I launched into an unscripted, unchoreographed, and exceedingly vigorous jig. Back home in the States, such a reaction might well have prompted laughter from any bystanders, or even gained me a few seconds on *America's Funniest Home Videos.*

Boris wasn't laughing. He had also, I noticed through the excruciating discomfort, retreated well back from the tree, taking my wide-eyed companion with him.

Realizing that no one from the New York Ballet was around to grade my potential and wholly involuntary audition, I stopped jumping about like a madman. Clenching my teeth, I searched for the source of the fiery pain. In the center of the back of my left hand, one of those tiny ants was busily screwing itself abdomen- and stinger-first into my flesh, rotating its entire body like a tiny organic drill. It took several forceful shoves with the edge of my other hand to finally dislodge the ant. While the miniscule arthropod that had inflicted the pain had been dealt with, the fire remained. It did not go away, in fact, for a couple of days. Not until the inflamed red spot the size of a dime that marked the injection site finally faded from sight.

Coming over, Boris eyed the angry-looking redness appraisingly.

"I have some salve if you want to put something on it."

"No, I'll be all right," I told him. What I didn't say was, *I'll tolerate it for as long as it lasts in order to remind me of my arrogance.*

It is said that when the local natives want to severely punish someone, they tie them naked to a tangarana tree. I feel safe in presuming that if the miscreant so condemned doesn't die, they are suitably chastised for the rest of their life. I know from experience what one sting can do.

I prefer not to imagine what a hundred or so would feel like.

* * *

Northeastern Gabon, January 2007

IN THE MOUNTAINOUS NORTHEASTERN CORNER of the central African nation of Gabon, in a region noticed, if at all, by the rest of the world for its occasional headline-making outbreaks of the deadly Ebola virus, lies an Eden-like clearing in the jungle called Langoué Bai. Made famous by *National Geographic* explorer J. Michael Fay in the course of his trail-blazing mega-transect of central Africa, Langoué Bai is home to forest elephants, sitatungas, lowland gorillas, and other fabulous beasts. My sister, Carol, had always wanted to see gorillas, while I dreamed of seeing elephants on a beach. Gabon is the only place in the world where the latter encounter is reasonably possible. Having successfully encountered the surreal sand-loving pachyderms on the coast in Loango National Park, we were now on our way inland to Langoué.

The *bai* (the Bayaka word for an opening in the forest) lay in rugged and undeveloped Ivindo National Park. To get to Ivindo, we took the train from the town of Libreville. Winding its way through the heart of Africa, the Trans-Gabon train is a little-known miracle of engineering. Its front cars also boast air-conditioning so powerful that it threatens to turn the upper-class passengers into Gabonsicles. In the days to come, we would have occasion to recall that over-cranked air-con longingly.

The town of Ivindo would not exist except to serve the logging industry. An undisciplined scattering of homes, small bars, and shops fan out from the train station side of the railroad tracks. Met by operatives from the Wildlife Conservation Society that operates the scientific station inside Ivindo and that occasionally welcomes tourists, we and a young couple from San Francisco on their honeymoon (!) tossed our backpacks into the rear of a big, dirt-caked 4x4 and embarked on the nearly five-hour drive to the trailhead.

You know when you've reached the end of the line because the road grows progressively worse and the vegetation ever denser around it until the track simply slams up against a steep jungle-covered slope and stops. In the rainy season, the dirt road is virtually impassable. Climbing gratefully out of the vehicle after the long, jouncing ride, we immediately found ourselves in the company of swarms of bees. After a minute or two of near-panic engendered by thoughts of Africanized bees, it became apparent that we were in no real danger. These weren't Africanized bees: They were just African bees.

All right, so maybe I'm splitting antennae here, but it was clear the hundreds of happy honey hunters buzzing all around us were not interested in us—only in any open food, drink, or other exotic foodstuffs that we might have imported into their neighborhood. They landed on us, got tangled in our hair, and explored our clothes, all without anyone suffering so much as a single sting.

While my sister and I did our best to ignore the clouds of peripatetic pollen pickers, the rest of our party loaded supplies onto their backs preparatory to setting off. There are no roads to the Ivindo scientific station, no airstrip, not even room enough to land a helicopter. Food, medicine, scientific equipment, computers, furniture—everything goes in or comes out on the back of a porter. As the column formed up, I felt as if I was stepping back in time to the Africa of a hundred years ago, when every expedition's equipment was transported overland on the backs of hired porters. In contrast to my imaginings, the digital watches and occasional rock T-shirt the men wore placed them firmly in the present day.

It is a seven-hour walk (for a healthy human being in acceptable physical condition) from the trailhead to the research station. Much of this is uphill, with the worst part being the first few miles. Steep, muddy, and hacked out of raw hillside jungle, it's a tough enough march in good weather. In rain, it inculcates twisted ankles and broken bones. Thankfully, the only moisture we had to contend with was preserved in the mud, in small puddles of standing water, and in the perspiration that was already streaming down our bodies.

Our relief was unrestrained when we were told we had reached the top of the "hill" and that while more upslope remained, it would be nothing like what we had just conquered. Thus refreshed in spirit if not in body, we resumed the trek.

"Stop."

Like the porters, our lead guide was a member of a local tribe. I moved up to stand alongside him and follow his gaze into the jungle ahead. The rain forest here was comparatively open. Large trees atop the plateau were more widely spaced than what we had encountered at the bottom of the canyon. This allowed more sunlight to reach the forest floor, resulting in a greater profusion of bushes and other lesser growths. My gaze fell somewhat, and my attention was drawn to what I first took to be a trick of the sunlight.

The forest floor appeared to be in motion.

"Driver ants." The guide flashed a learned smile. "Do you know what to do?"

I knew army ants and tangarana ants and their cousins from South and Central America, but this was the first time I had been confronted with their Old World counterparts. Furthermore, this immense colony was not marching, but foraging. That meant that instead of moving in a single, rigid, predictable column, easy enough to avoid or simply jump over, they had spread out over a wide area. Its limits were defined, but extensive. The underbrush was too thick and the ground still too steep and uneven to allow us to go around the colony. Besides, in hunting mode, the ants would be on every trunk, branch, and leaf. Pushing through the brush meant one would inevitably get them on hands, torso—maybe even one's face.

The glistening red bodies completely covered the trail ahead of us and extended far into the forest on both sides. I admitted to our guide that no, I did not know what to do, and if he had any suggestions for how best to avoid the nightmare swarm directly in front of us, I would gladly take them.

"Avoid?" His expression turned querulous. "Too difficult, take too long. This is what you do."

Turning from me, he rushed forward and sprinted straight down the ant-carpeted section of trail. The distance from one side of the foraging colony to the other was at least ten yards. Halting on the far side, once again on an ant-free section of the track, he paused to slap and pick at himself.

My sister had come up alongside me. Carol had shown her mettle and determination ever since our transfer flight from Douala, Cameroon, to Port-Gentil, Gabon, on an otherwise empty Dornier through a raging tropical thunderstorm. She was game for anything. But she was from Orange County, California, and dashing through a million or so ferociously feeding driver ants was not an option that had appeared in any of the tourist brochures I had forwarded to her prior to our departure. She eyed the swarm dubiously.

"We're supposed to *run* through that?"

I looked at her. "Unless you want to walk."

She responded to my sarcasm with an expression that was wholly devoid of amusement.

Bending over, I tucked the hem of each leg of my pants into my boots. The day before leaving home I had treated boots, socks, and clothing with permethrin, a flower-derived natural insecticide that works fairly well at repelling ticks, chiggers, and other hungry small critters that like to crawl up one's legs. Among those insects it was supposed to dissuade, I did not recall seeing on the can any specific mention of African driver ants, but at the time I was not in a position to query the manufacturer as to its product's efficacy in deterring that particular insect.

In any event, I was about to find out.

Making sure my pack was securely on my back, I took a deep breath and ran, trying to make as little contact with the ground as possible. *Long strides*, I told myself. *On tiptoes. And whatever you do . . .*

Don't fall down.

I made it across without suffering a single sting or bite. My satisfaction vanished a moment later when the ants that had climbed aboard while studiously ignoring the permethrin managed to somehow get inside my pant legs and set to work. It wasn't too bad. Nothing like the tangarana-ant sting I had suffered in Peru. *Of course*, I told myself, *magnified a few thousand times over, the burning discomfort I was enduring would probably be somewhat less tolerable.* My sister, I am happy to report, did wonderfully well.

We encountered three or four more such swarms before reaching the station. They were still there on the trail days later to greet us on the long walk back down. Each time I ran, I tried to maneuver differently. Each time, no matter what I did, I still suffered a few stings and bites.

No matter how hard you try, you cannot avoid the ground when it is alive.

* * *

Southeastern Peru, July 1998

MORE THAN A DECADE PASSED before I was able to return to Manú. In the interim, I had visited dozens of countries including Gabon, but my memories of southeastern Peru were strong and I had always determined to go back. Eleven years sees many changes on our crowded planet, even in a place as remote as the Madre de Dios region. The nearest real town, Puerto Maldonado, had grown from a collection of tin-roofed shacks linked together by a network of dirt tracks into a thriving regional hub. Boca Manú, which I remembered as little more than a couple of huts poised tenuously at the confluence of the Alto Madre de Dios and the Manú Rivers, had become an actual small town. There was a new establishment just outside the park boundary and Boris's dream lodge had long since been opened for business. Though still thankfully infrequent, tourist canoes now plied the Manú River itself on predetermined schedules.

I was elated to reacquaint myself with the region surrounding the still unspoiled Cocha Salvador. This time, I had the pleasure of sleeping in a screened-in room with a bed instead of on a sleeping bag in a rotting tent. Meals prepared in a kitchen and served at wooden tables made recollections of eating while standing up in *la casa de los mosquitos* seem like a memory from an ancient fable. The nocturnal horror of the pit toilet was all in the past, and showers were available. All sheer luxury compared to my former visit.

One thing fortunately remained unchanged and untouched, however, and that was the surrounding primeval rain forest.

When I declared that I wished to take solitary walks in the forest, I was met with unease by the concerned lodge staff. With a knowing smile, I explained that I had walked the shores of this lake when there had been no buildings here, and that I knew what I was doing. After eleven more years spent traveling the world, I did know better. If nothing else, I had learned enough not to let myself get overconfident even in seemingly safe surrounds.

For example, the first rule to remember while walking through rain forest and jungle is simple: No matter how attractive something is, no matter how much you may think you know about it be it plant or animal or unidentifiable, assume that everything you encounter can bite, sting, or otherwise hurt you.

With that caution in mind, I took my walks alone, reveling in the sounds and sights of the forest, free from the enervating chatter of visiting housewives and day-tripping tourists. I saw much that I had seen before and plenty that was new. Back at the lodge, I cheerfully discussed my encounters with the staff guides whenever they could spare a little time to sit and chat.

I was especially fond of the conversations I had with an energetic young female guide who I will call Anna. She had committed to the lodge for a year, following which paid sojourn she hoped to return to Lima to further her studies in tropical biology. We were sitting and talking one day when she happened to ask, "Is there anything you'd like to see that you haven't seen? I mean, besides a jaguar or a harpy eagle or something really difficult?"

I thought a moment. "Yes. I'd like to see an isula ant nest."

She blanched. I always thought that was purely a literary description of someone's reaction, but you could see her actually go a little pale. I had expected a response, but not one quite so strong. I hastened to reassure her.

"I'll be careful, I promise. I know the isula ant. I won't take any chances."

She hesitated a moment longer before nodding reluctantly. "OK. As long as you promise. I know you've been here before, but as a guest I'm still responsible for you."

"I won't do anything stupid."

She rose from the rattan chair. "I actually know where there's one not too far from here."

Those who have never spent time in real rain forest assume that to see exotic and sometimes rare animals one has to spend days or at least hours traveling by canoe and hiking on foot. While this is true of certain specific locales like Langoué Bai in Gabon, in many other instances it's a misnomer propounded by decades of television nature documentaries in which the suffering of the photographers to get the picture is emphasized in order to add drama to the process. Cutting back and forth from the subject plant or animal to a cameraman or woman sitting motionless in a blind can get pretty boring, and is as devoid of action as it is of the human interest so beloved of sponsors and their ratings monitors. Far more drama is to be had from watching people stumble through raging jungle streams, or rappel down rugged mountainsides, or shimmy up liana-draped trees. All of this does happen, of course, and sometimes it's unavoidable in the course of conducting real science, but it's not always the only way to see interesting things.

I remember spending a week in Ecuador's fabulous Yasuní National Park trying to catch a glimpse of the park's signature species, the golden-mantled tamarin. Like all small primates, this spectacular small monkey is not easy to see. Both on my own and in the company of the lodge's guides I spent days searching for them, each time without success.

It was my last morning at the Napo Wildlife Center. The other handful of guests were all birders and were out in the forest busily indulging in the orgy of aves spotting that was their chosen passion. Yasuní is considered one of the best places in the world for birding. Birders are more obsessive about their pastime than a foot fetishist locked overnight in a Manolo Blahnik store. A jaguar could attack an anaconda directly behind them, and they would ignore it in their anxiety to identify the subspecies of parrot feeding on palm nuts that they happened to be observing.

Sitting alone on the open terrace of the lodge's restaurant, I heard a burst of idiosyncratic chittering. Thinking it was only some common monkeys, I nevertheless roused myself and walked out behind the lodge, following the noise.

Two tall trees behind the lodge were full of golden-mantled tamarins.

So much for slogging through canyons sloppy with mud and swarming with leeches in search of rare animals.

But back to Manú.

Anna and I had not gone a hundred yards from the camp when she turned slightly off the trail. Twenty feet or so back into the bush she stopped, began searching, and finally picked up a suitable fallen branch a yard long and half an inch thick. Studying the forest floor intently, I saw nothing unusual.

Slowly approaching a slightly built-up area of dirt located between the flaring buttress roots of a mature cecropia, she inserted one end of the stick into a small, dark hole at the top of the gently sloping dirt pile. She then proceeded to jab the stick sharply down into the opening three, four, five times.

A black shape emerged from the hole. Then another, and another.

She threw the stick aside and retreated. Fast. Their energy sapped by the unrelenting heat and humidity, people tend to move slowly in the rain forest. To this day, I don't believe I've seen anyone move as fast in such sweltering surroundings as Anna did at that moment. Halting about ten feet away from the tree, she alternated her attention between the creatures that were now boiling out of the hole and me. I had insisted that I would not do anything stupid, but she was taking no chances.

Emerging angrily from their home were some fifteen to twenty *Paraponera clavata*. When compared to the hordes of army ants easily encountered anywhere in the Amazon, or the driver ants of tropical Africa, that may not sound like much of an eruption. Except the representatives of this genus are the biggest ants in the world.

Known in Peru as isula ants, some specimens of *Paraponera* are reputed to grow as long as two inches. Their hefty, ruthlessly efficient bodies look like they have been welded together out of shards of reddish black steel. Their jaws alone are longer than many species of ant. Solitary hunters, they haul everything from other ants to grasshoppers and even frogs and salamanders back to their nest, which unlike that of many ants is not dominated by a queen. The isula ant is the Spartan of the ant world, irresistible in single combat, a Hymenopteran Praetorian guard. The mastodon ant.

In other parts of South America, the isula ant is known as the bullet ant, because if you are stung by one it supposedly feels as if you've been shot. Elsewhere it is often called the twenty-four-hour ant, because the excruciating pain of its sting can last for a full day and nothing can mitigate the suffering.

Moving closer, I took care while aiming my camera. Every couple of minutes, a concerned Anna would say something like, "That's close enough," or "Be careful," or most tellingly, "Watch your feet." She didn't have to warn me. Thanks to a single encounter with the tangarana ant, I had learned my lesson eleven years earlier. The tangarana ant that had stung me so forcefully had been about the size of an isula ant compound eye.

Spreading out, the agitated ants began to search for the source of whatever had disturbed their nest. In their determination and purpose, they were fascinating to watch. On their bodies, details of ant anatomy that usually have to be studied under a magnifying glass or microscope were easily visible to the naked eye. Powerful jaws long enough to be measured with a ruler opened and snapped shut expectantly.

I know what you're thinking. This is the part where I feel a stabbing pain in my leg or arm. This is the section where I lie in bed writhing in agony for the next twenty-four hours, decrying my rashness at getting so close to such a small but deadly carnivore, lamenting my inability to see the attack coming.

Sorry.

Glancing down and away from the camera, I noticed a single isula ant actively exploring the ground near my left boot. Another was nearby. I could have raised my foot and crushed each of them into the ground. Revenge for the tangarana ant attack of more than a decade ago. Revenge in Nature, however, has neither place nor meaning. It is purely a human conceit, and one to which I was not about to succumb.

I switched off the camera and stepped back. Still watching me closely, Anna was visibly relieved and more than happy to leave the vicinity of the nest to the patrolling ants. There are times and places in which I will take chances or push the envelope a little, but as I assured Anna, I do not do anything overtly dumb.

My incredibly understanding wife, of course, would sigh knowingly and beg to differ.

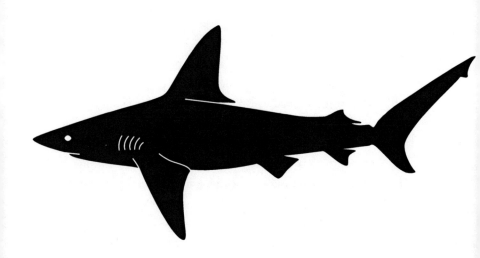

VI

SHARKS I HAVEN'T JUMPED

Bismarck Sea, September 1997

I'M OFTEN ASKED WHICH OF all the places I have visited is my favorite. The question is impossible to answer because one inevitably ends up trying to compare apples to oranges. Actually, apples are more comparable to oranges than Italy is to Indonesia, or Brussels to Burkina Faso. I can contrast Rome with Madrid, or Yekaterinburg with Chicago, but not Peru with Prague.

Every place I have ever been has something to recommend it; every person I have ever met something to commend them. Or as my wife succinctly puts it, "You have no taste: You like everyplace and everybody." To this assertion, I must plead mostly guilty.

While it is impossible to offer an all-inclusive answer to the query, it is possible to break down encounters into categories. For walking, my favorites would be Manhattan and London. For history, Prague and Rome. For sheer surprise, Istanbul. For animal life, South Africa. For Nature in the raw, Namibia, Gabon, and Peru. The most beautiful natural places I have seen on Earth are the immeasurably vast Grand Canyon of Arizona, the Tolkienesque Lofoten Islands of Norway, Venezuela's otherworldly Canaima National Park, the untouched underwater marvels of West Papua, and my number-one choice, the incomparable Iguazú Falls on the border between Argentina and Brazil.

But for an all-around, utterly fascinating, highly diverse step back in time, the prize goes hands-down to Papua New Guinea.

This is a land replete with spectacular sights both above and below the water. Vibrant with amazing human cultures that have survived largely unchanged for thousands of years, swarming with remarkable animals, it can boast whole regions that have yet to be touched by Western civilization. There is simply no place like it left on Earth.

Among its unrivaled attractions, up in the Bismarck Sea north of the large, lush island of New Hanover, there used to be a place of magic called Silvertip Reef.

Sharks, I try to explain to the querulous who know them only from what they have seen in film and on television, are no different from dogs. Leave a shark alone, and it will behave very much like any neighborhood pooch. Encountering a stranger, it sizes them up, tries to take a sniff or two, attempts to ascertain if you qualify as either a danger (swim away!) or potential food (sniff harder), and eventually reaches a decision based on these observations. Dump a tub of blood and fish guts into the water in close proximity to curious sharks, and you sometimes are rewarded with what has melodramatically been labeled a "feeding frenzy."

Now try this. Go to your local butcher. Buy twenty pounds of raw hamburger, complete with juices. Find an alley. Look for a pack of dogs. Toss the hamburger into their midst. You'll get the same reaction impatient photographers do when slopping chum to sharks, only with a frenzy of legs instead of fins.

Regrettably, because of the way they look and are perceived to behave, certain creatures have always had a bad press. Sharks unquestionably. Among other similarly cuteness-impaired species can also be counted spiders, snakes, and rats. If not for spiders, we would be drowning in insects. If not for snakes, the planet's pesky rodent population would be far more difficult to deal with. As for rats, they are intelligent, family-oriented, and make excellent pets. I'm sure if you asked them, not one would speak up to declare proudly, "Hey, we *like* being infested with fleas that carry bubonic plague! Chipmunks do, too, and *they* aren't subject to universal condemnation!"

That's because unlike run-of-the-mill rodents, chipmunks are perceived by humans to be . . . cute. Even though they're just rats with racing stripes.

As if we humans didn't carry diseases of our own. If gorillas understood biology well enough, at the sight of every approaching cluster of camera-wielding human tourists, they would immediately begin screaming, "Run, everybody, run! It's those filthy measles-transmitting humans again!"

Perception is not the same as understanding. Therefore, spare a thought for the poor shark, which performs its role of top predator sans the kudos and admiration the handsome lion and sensuous tiger claim effortlessly as their birthright.

There are 360 species of shark, from the ten-inch-long spined pygmy shark to the largest fish in the ocean, the forty-foot, fifteen-ton whale shark. As if further proof was needed that Nature indeed has a sense of humor, the pygmy shark will bite while its gigantic cousin will not. In fact, I can attest that if you scratch a juvenile whale shark under its enormous, plankton-swilling mouth, it will go vertical in the water and hang there like a contented puppy until you tire of caressing it. Just don't try to catch a mature one by its tail, which will knock you aside as effortlessly and indifferently as a teenager flicking a half-eaten Cheeto at a friend in history class.

Below the whale shark and considerably above the spined pygmy shark in size are a number of strikingly attractive sharks that boast of no-nonsense dentition. I've already spoken of the great white. A step down from this master of the seas are the hammerhead, the tiger shark, and *Carcharhinus albimarginatus*, the silvertip shark. Growing to a length of more than ten feet and weighing in at more than 350 pounds, the silvertip is virtually a poster child for everyone's idea of the classic shark: sleek, beautifully proportioned, and active. Silvertip distribution is worldwide in many of the tropical seas.

Silvertip Reef in northern Papua New Guinea got its name not only because the eponymous shark could frequently be encountered there, but because the occasional scuba operation to reach this isolated corner of the ocean discovered that the sharks could be acclimated to recognize when they were about to be fed by visitors. So along with the usual assortment of victuals intended to keep their passengers properly nourished, the infrequent dive boats that visited this location developed the habit of including among their supplies a suitably attractive mishmash of tasty shark snacks.

In our case, this consisted of a steel oil drum full of frozen fish parts too rank, slimy, tasteless, bony, or organ-rich to meet the minimum specifications of even the most undiscriminating pet food manufacturer. In other words, to a shark, chateaubriand.

Every one of us on the *Tiata* had heard about Silvertip Reef long before we anchored there. For several of the divers on board, it was the principal reason they had signed on for the current itinerary. Though we had enjoyed superb diving for more than a week in the vicinity of the main islands of New Ireland and New Hanover, including a rare visit to the remote Tingwon Islands, the promise of Silvertip Reef and everything we had heard about it had never strayed far from our thoughts. And now, we were there.

As we assembled in the dining room for the usual predive briefing, it was clear from Captain Dave's uncharacteristically somber attitude and expression that the forthcoming dive would be different in a number of respects from those that had preceded it. His usual jauntiness was absent, his gaze noticeably more intent. We were not going into the water to look for sea horses or to take pretty pictures of batfish and purple chromis. Not this time.

"The sharks may already be here," he told us. "They've learned to recognize the sound of the boat's engines and connect it with a feed. They might well be right under your fins as you jump in. Once you're in the water and have checked out your gear, ignore them and head straight down to the reef. Find yourself a spot and settle in. No hanging around in mid-water." He paused for emphasis. "That's where they expect to find the food. As soon as everyone is in place, we'll drop the barrel's contents." He scanned the cabin. "Any questions?"

We looked at one another. Nobody said anything. We were eager and anxious in equal measure. The captain nodded, gratified that we understood.

Cameras were prepared, checked, and passed sternward in silence. One by one, we slipped into our bc's (bouyancy compensators—the gear-laden vests you see on scuba divers), hefted our tanks, and executed giant-stride entries off the edge of the stern dive platform. The instant I hit the warm water, I let go of my mask and regulator and looked down.

There they were: three big, husky, gorgeous silvertips, circling effortlessly directly beneath us. No gray reef sharks these, no nervous little resident whitetips. Had they been great whites . . .

Had they been great whites, of course, no one would have been jumping into the water.

We sank down, everyone trying to look in three dimensions at once. As we descended, more silvertips arrived. Five, six—within minutes of our hitting the water, there were eight of them carouseling around and among us. Our presence was noted—you could see the golden eyes with their black pupils following your every move. But otherwise, we were ignored. Edible we might be, but our shapes were all wrong, as was our smell. Shark wary of human and human wary of shark, together we infused the ridgelike reef with an almost palpable aura of mutual respect. With each diver locating a place where there was little or no live coral, we settled down and waited for the show to begin.

When dumped over the side of the *Tiata*, the frozen-solid contents of the chum barrel made a much bigger splash than I expected. Recognizing the by-now familiar sound, the sharks instantly homed in on the slowly descending and rapidly defrosting cylindrical mass and began to tear it to pieces. The faster it thawed in the eighty-three-degree water, the more swiftly it was consumed. Not every shark attacked the sinking glob simultaneously. They were excited and somewhat agitated, but methodical in their assault. There was no panic among them, no fighting, and certainly no "feeding frenzy."

After a while, two things became clear to those of us looking on: The sharks were in no great hurry to feed or had already consumed a share of the spoils, and they were quite comfortable with our proximity. Perhaps more so than several of us with them. During the briefing, we had been told (warned?) that having become acclimated to the presence of divers, they might approach us more closely than was customary for their species. Also that they might be just as likely to eat their fill and then swim off into the blue.

We were not told, however, just how close they might come.

Having a brawny eight-foot shark pass within arm's reach of you is one thing when you are in a protective cage and the shark is outside. The feeling is utterly different when there are no bars separating you from one of Nature's most perfect predators. The shark's eye looks at you, you look back at the shark. It is not an intelligent eye like that of a mammal or a cephalopod. It is not cold and unfeeling so much as it is alien, otherworldly. You realize as you meet its gaze that there is *something* going on behind that eye, but whatever it is will remain forever beyond your ken. Above all, there is an overriding sense of awareness of your presence. You are being speculated upon. You are being sized up. To a shark, you can be one of two things: a threat, or food. Above all, you realize that this is not a movie, the shark is not an actor or a computer-generated image or an animatronic puppet being propelled by a motor and directed by off-screen handlers, and you are not at home sitting on your couch munching popcorn while watching the Discovery Channel.

A shark can strike as fast as a snake. This is a fact better understood in the abstract than in reality.

So beautiful, so graceful. The idea of killing such a magnificent animal just for its fins while leaving the rest to rot and die is one any sentient mind should not be capable of accepting, though all-too many humans do. My wife and I have cats and dogs. I once had a boa constrictor. Occasionally, a cat or dog will nip a visitor. The snake never did.

What about a shark? And not just any shark, but a serious shark like the silvertip?

I looked around. Visibility on the isolated reef verged on unlimited. As is my preference at such times, I was off a little ways by myself. No one was watching me. That was hardly surprising, with eight silvertips circulating steadily among us. Movement in the water made me look to my left. One was coming straight toward me. Several had already done so, passing as close to where I was crouching as college friends in a crowded bar. Swimming slowly and without concern, its tail moving back and forth like a metronome to propel it through the water, the silvertip passed directly over my head. Its white belly gleamed like buffed fiberglass.

There are moments in our lives when we do something we have often thought about doing but never really expected to do. When such an occasion actually arrives, the time for acting on impulse usually lasts little more than a second or two. Spend time in judicious contemplation of the action itself and in a wink the opportunity is gone, usually forever.

Extending myself slightly, I reached up and let my bare fingertips trail along the silvertip's underside. The flesh was firm to the touch, like a tire. Surprised but not unsettled by the contact, the silvertip gave a wider twitch of its tail and accelerated slightly.

That was all. That was everything.

Later, out of the water and back on the boat, Captain Dave confronted me privately. Everyone else was otherwise occupied, having doffed their dive gear and retired to their cabins or gathered excitedly around the coffeemaker to discuss the remarkable encounter they had just experienced.

"I saw what you did." His tone was accusatory.

I protested. "It was OK. I was careful, and gentle. I've been around plenty of sharks." I did not add that I was not in the habit of stroking them.

He nodded thoughtfully. "Just don't do it again." And then he added, because I was a paying passenger and he preferred to advise and not command, "Please?"

His request was moot because the opportunity did not arise again. We were given one dive at Silvertip Reef and one only. It was the last real dive of our trip before we returned to Kavieng. Understandably, the dive boat operators who managed to get out this far always saved Silvertip Reef for last because they knew that no matter how good or bad all the preceding dives had been, a visit to the reef would by itself be sufficient to make any diver's trip a great one.

Many years passed before I happened to hear that the wonders of Silvertip Reef were no more. Learning of its secret, a group of local fishermen had gone out with chum, drawn in the sharks, and caught and killed every one of them, probably just for their fins. I think I remember crying when I read that. Having seen a great deal of serious poverty and severe hardship around the world, it's hard for me to judge and condemn such actions. But this was one instance in which I could not help myself.

* * *

Silvertips may be the dominant shark in the Bismarck Sea, but that doesn't mean you should ignore the others. On a dive close to the island of New Ireland, I suddenly found myself fighting an unexpectedly strong shallow-water current. While my fellow divers successfully descended and made their way along a deep reef line, I was picked up, swept backward, and carried away from them. While I enjoy being on my own underwater, I do not like being caught up in currents I can't swim against.

Like a good swimmer, a good diver knows that you don't fight a current. The ocean being somewhat bigger and stronger than the most powerful swimmer, it's not only futile but dangerous to try and battle it head-on. Swim sideways out of the current, or look for something to hold on to, or drift with it until you can safely surface and call for help.

There was no reason to panic. The current was propelling me along the outer edge of our chosen reef. At worst, I could surface and swim to one of two nearby islets. The dive boat itself was not far away. So I relaxed and, like a commuter on a train, watched the world go by.

It turned out that a certain segment of the world going by was also watching me.

There were six of them. Juvenile gray reef sharks, the largest no more than three feet long. Not exactly Jaws, but not domesticated koi, either. They were following me in single file, for all the world like boys trailing their scoutmaster. I kept an eye on them as I enjoyed my colorful surroundings. At any moment, I expected them to become bored and peel off in search of more interesting and easily consumable intruders. They did not.

They were still with me when I started to run low on air. Having half a dozen young sharks tracking you while you are submerged only adds to the beauty and exoticism of your surroundings. Having them interested in you while you are stuck floating on the surface is another matter entirely.

The current had finally succumbed to the influence of the nearby islands, allowing me to maneuver more freely. Before I surfaced and hailed the pickup boat, I decided something had to be done about my persistent entourage. Coming to a deliberate halt, I hovered in some twenty feet of water and glared at the first teenager in line. The group immediately broke apart.

And began to circle me.

The near-perfect ring, myself in the center, incongruously put me in mind of old western movies. I was the wagon train, the sharks the circling Apaches. Except the only thing they were shooting at me were cold, fishy glances, and I had nothing with which to respond. For a crazed moment, I considered wildly waving my arms at them and yelling, "Shoo, shark, shoo!" As this was not a technique I could recall recommended in any marine handbook I had read, I forbore from acting like a fool and kept my arms close to my sides. But I admit I was tempted.

Meanwhile, the readout on my dive computer that indicated the amount of air remaining in my tank continued its inexorable progression toward zero.

I was down to a couple of hundred pounds per square inch when I realized I had to find a way to discourage the sharks or else I would be forced to surface with them still encircling me. Banging on my tank was more likely to attract additional sharky spectators than drive these away. Rushing them was more likely to frighten them off than provoke an attack—but while the likelihood of such an action being successful was in my favor, it was not a certainty. I was not in Las Vegas. The prospective gamble involved teeth, not tokens.

Hoping for a quick pickup from the dive boat, I decided to surface while I still had some air left in my tank. Spreading my arms and legs wide to make myself look as big as possible, I started upward.

The instant I did so, the sharks turned and swam off.

Having completed my safety stop and returned to the surface, I dipped my face back into the water to anxiously scan my immediate surroundings. Not one of the juvenile gray reefs remained within view. My toes, and the rest of me, were safe. I went from feeling mildly threatened to feeling slightly foolish.

Most people know what a puppy's toy feels like, but it's not often one gets the chance to know what it feels like to be one.

* * *

As I mentioned previously, when great white shark experts and guides Rodney and Andrew Fox put out chunks of tuna or mackerel around their boat to keep visiting great whites interested and available for viewing, the pieces of fish were attached to one or two balloons to keep them floating at the surface. These were not specialized great-white-watching gear, but ordinary party balloons purchased at a local store. I retain a vivid memory of one great white that had taken our bait cruising by my cage with a bright blue child's balloon trailing on a string from the right side of its mouth. The balloon and the length of twine attached to it soon took their leave of the patrolling animal, but in my mind that particular great white will forever be ignominiously remembered as the clown shark.

Largely because of the plethora of bloodthirsty television documentaries in which they are featured, people rarely, if ever, associate sharks with humor. Of the few artists who regularly draw amusement from the actions of *Carcharodon* and its relatives, the most notable is Jim Toomey of the widely syndicated cartoon strip *Sherman's Lagoon*. In this he was preceded, frequently and to much mirth, by the inimitable Gary Larson's *The Far Side*. In addition to sharks, Larson extracted dry and frequently skewed humor from both the animal and plant kingdoms, places where humans were often reduced to little more than bipedal straight lines. I'm pretty sure I've seen, and enjoyed, every cartoon Gary Larson ever drew. I never thought I'd find myself acting in one. . . .

* * *

West Australia, April 1992

MORE THAN HALF THE POPULATION of Australia lives in or near its five largest cities. Not for nothing is the rest of the country called the Outback. The Outback itself is broken down into smaller, though still enormous, subregions with names of their own. The Top End, for example, refers to the finger of land that points toward New Guinea. In the vast northwest of the continent lie the districts of the Pilbara and the Kimberley. An area the size of Great Britain, the Kimberley is home to barely enough people to populate a good-size American or European town. It's an enormous, often dry, sometimes cyclone-swept region of spinifex scrub, exotic animals, descendents of the continent's first human settlers, spectacular sheer-sided gorges, unique insects, and a rugged rust-red coastline that is as magnificent as it is unpopulated.

We were heading north along this coast after having paused to photograph and film the famed whale sharks of Ningaloo Reef. The purpose of the voyage was to allow Brent Mills of Nature Films (based in Chattanooga, Tennessee) to produce a documentary on Rodney Fox. Having previously written two articles for *National Geographic* magazine on this little-known and visually dramatic part of Australia, Rodney wanted to revisit the area without the pressure of having to write to a deadline. This coincided neatly with Brent's desire to make a documentary about him, and so the expedition was born.

I was invited to participate because—well, to this day I'm not exactly sure why I was invited to participate. Partly, I think, it was because Rodney and I got along well. Partly, because he knew I shared his enthusiasm for such exploration. And partly, perhaps, because on a previous journey he may have sensed that I can get along with most anyone under nearly any circumstances. The latter is a facility not to be undervalued when one is to be packed into a too-small, inadequate boat with a bunch of strangers for an un-air-conditioned tropical journey of a month's duration.

The rest of the production team was a decidedly mixed bunch. There was a professional underwater photographer, much of whose previous work had been in, amusingly, Antarctica. Joining Rodney was his remarkable wife, Kay. The crew consisted of the boat's owner and captain plus his irrepressible mate and all-around deckhand. Brent Mills was joined by a good friend of his, Robbie Lauren Kyle Mantooth, scion of another notable Chattanooga family. One of the kindest and most beautiful young women I have ever met, she was also the expedition's official still photographer. Not long after the expedition, she moved to Hollywood and willingly surrounded herself with carnivores of a species whose predatory habits and lifestyle it is not within the scope of this particular book to describe. Looking back over the years, I have a feeling that deep down she was more at home with the fish.

As for Brent, through no fault of his own, he was a representative of a subgroup of humanity that I often find it difficult to deal with: people who inherit money. However, in his case, a more amiable and almost self-consciously self-effacing individual would be hard to imagine. He was kindly and considerate to a fault, which I think sometimes resulted in people taking advantage of him. But his dedication to the project at hand was assured and unbreakable.

Finding a boat and a captain willing to forgo usual business to take off for a month's expedition up what many would consider to be the most dangerous coast in Australia, a place that boasts the second highest tidal shifts in the world after Canada's Bay of Fundy, had proven a difficult challenge even for Rodney. Normally employed for fishing charters, the *Nordon* left many things to be desired, most notable of which was a complete lack of internal climate control. In the fierce Australian sun, the only relief from the boat's stifling interior was to be had out on deck while the boat was in motion. And at times, various members of the expedition found the only way they could get any rest was to move outside and sleep on deck.

Brent's footage of visiting whale sharks at Ningaloo was stunning (Eugenie Clark and a formal *National Geographic* crew arrived there several weeks after us), and the conditions on board notwithstanding, everyone was in good spirits as we set a course northward along the coast. We paused to visit the Montebello Islands where the British had carried out nuclear weapons' testing in the 1950s. Rodney and I were the only ones willing to dive there. As I recall, this had something to do with a proprietary concern among the younger members of the expedition regarding the future viability of eggs and sperm. Those who didn't dive missed little. Rodney and I encountered virtually no life on the bomb-blasted seafloor save for the occasional enormous and isolated oyster. All through the following week, these gargantuan shellfish provided excellent fodder for innumerable jokes focusing on radioactive mutant oysters. Also for a pot of Rodney's fresh oyster stew, which— I regret to say—came out awful. At least, no one glowed following consumption.

Continuing on up the coast, we stopped at isolated towns and outposts to take on fresh water and fuel. I remember a bikini-clad Robbie and her friend, a distance runner from Virginia, pausing on an industrial dock to take an extended outdoor freshwater shower. This unassuming girlish interlude succeeded in bringing a sizable commercial operation to a complete halt as every goggle-eyed employee within eyeball range (and a couple who hurriedly managed to locate binoculars) stopped everything they were doing to watch.

Eventually, we reached Broome, the only community of any size on the entire Kimberley coast, where we laid over for a couple of days to rest and reprovision for the remainder of the journey north.

Here, I must beg your indulgence for a moment as I find myself compelled to relate an anecdote involving ice cream.

Old-town Broome was largely deserted on the morning I decided to take a sightseeing stroll. Every other member of the expedition was at a local hotel, luxuriating in the presence of air-conditioned rooms and ice and other modern amenities. I found myself wandering alone among the single-story buildings, passed the closed Paspaley pearl showroom, and in the simmering heat eventually found myself confronting a mirage. It had to be a mirage.

But this mirage was open for business.

It was a small establishment, nothing fancy, with a windowless entrance opening directly onto the street. An ice cream shop. Had it been the hottest Hollywood starlet-of-the-moment half-closing her eyes and beckoning to me with pursed lips, I could not have made a more determined beeline for it.

As the owner, a short but stout sunburned Aussie, waited patiently, I forced myself to take time enough to thoroughly peruse the neatly printed menu board that hung from the ceiling just inside the unshuttered opening.

"You've got coffee ice cream?"

"Yes," he replied, gracefully forbearing from chiding me for vocalizing the obvious.

"Could I get a coffee milk shake? Double-thick," I remembered to add. In Australia, if you ask for a milk shake, you get a drink made only with milk and flavoring. To have one made with ice cream, you need to ask for a double-thick.

Turning from me, the proprietor began to assemble the necessary ingredients to combine in a tall, steel mixing container. Looking on, I struggled to control my flow of saliva. Those of us on the *Nordon* had not had ice cream or anything like it for two weeks.

I soon noticed something that gave me pause.

"You're using vanilla ice cream."

He looked back at me. "That's right."

"But I asked for a coffee milk shake."

The man nodded. "All our double-thick milk shakes are made with vanilla ice cream, and then we add the appropriate flavoring."

I checked the overhead menu again, just to make sure. "But it says you have coffee ice cream. Couldn't you make mine with coffee ice cream?"

He shook his head. "We make all our double-thick milk shakes with vanilla ice cream and the chosen flavoring."

I implored. "I'll pay you double. Triple."

A sorrowful shake of the head. "Sorry, mate. That's not how we do it here."

I pondered this solemnly. "Well then, can I get a sundae made with coffee ice cream?"

The owner smiled back. "Sure thing."

"Good. This is what I'd like to do. I want to order a sundae made with coffee ice cream and a double-thick vanilla milk shake. Take the whipped cream, the nuts, the cherry for the sundae, and throw them away. Take the vanilla ice cream and throw *it* away. Then take the coffee ice cream for the sundae and put it in the milk-shake container with some milk and chocolate syrup, and mix it."

A steely-eyed Outback stare met mine. Surely, even Ned Kelly himself never lasered a more unswerving gaze upon an intended victim. The owner's tone firmed a little but otherwise did not change. "Sorry, mate— that's not how we do it here."

I caved. The milk shake made with vanilla ice cream and coffee syrup was refreshing enough—but somehow something had been lost, and not just in translation.

Two days later, fully equipped and laden with fuel, we headed out toward Rowley Shoals. These three perfect isolated atolls lie approximately 170 miles off the northwest coast of Australia. There is no vegetation on the sand cays that lie at the center of two of them. The water that separates Imperieuse, Clerke, and Mermaid Reefs from the mainland is deep and the currents between them strong, so no pollution or river run-off of any kind comes anywhere near the coral trio. Together, the three atolls comprise a marine park under government supervision. Regular patrols by aircraft are vital to ensure the protection of the sea life at the shoals from depredations by fishermen who attempt to sneak down from Indonesia in their sporadic efforts to poach the reefs' pristine stocks of giant clams (*Tridacna gigas*) and bêche-de-mer (*Isostichopus badionotus*) and to fish.

Rowley boasts the clearest water I have ever seen. Hovering just off the sandy bottom at a depth of more than sixty feet, I could easily count the number of fingers someone in a boat stuck over the side and into the water. I've experienced "unlimited" visibility in places like the Bismarck Sea, the eastern Tuamotus, and Micronesia, but for perfect visibility nothing compares to Rowley Shoals. Diving there was like swimming in air.

After several days of exploring and photographing, including a couple of amazing drift dives in the six-knot currents that periodically swept into the lagoons, it was decided to try and get some tiger shark footage featuring Rodney. Reports insisted that tigers were frequently seen at the shoals, and this would make an excellent coda to the film Brent was doubtless already editing together in his mind. Rodney, as always, was agreeable to the idea, though I think his wife, Kay, was less enthusiastic.

Nothing was left to chance. The perfectly transparent water minimized the likelihood of a surprise shark appearance. Descending to the sandy bottom at about seventy feet, both cameramen took up positions alongside shielding coral bommies. Situated more than ten yards apart from one another, these setups allowed for two completely different camera angles on their subject. Brent was with one cameraman, expedition still photographer Robbie with the other. Settling himself down twelve yards distant from and midway between the two camera locations, Rodney began steadily waving back and forth the half tuna he had brought with him, filling the otherwise clear water with the powerfully attractive scent of blood and fish oil.

Perhaps unsurprisingly, Kay and several others had elected to skip this particular dive and remain on the boat.

I wouldn't have missed it for anything. I also knew that my sole task was to stay out of the way. While everyone else was positioning themselves, I retreated to a ten-foot-high bulge of coral well to the rear of both camera positions and stayed there, just behind the crest of the ridge. From this position, I had a clear view of both camera setups and beyond them, of Rodney.

Five minutes passed. Ten. A couple of humongous potato cod arrived and proceeded to check out the unusual activity as somberly as a pair of undertakers methodically taking the measurements of a new client. Having examined the bubble-blowing interlopers and found them unremarkable, these impressive fish then took their leave, utterly unperturbed by the human intrusion. Shards of shattered rainbow, small reef fish darted in and out of the chum cloud, glorying in the unexpected source of fresh food.

Fifteen minutes. Still nothing. Not even a resident whitetip shark.

After twenty minutes of this, a visibly disappointed Brent gave the signal to wrap things up. Rodney ditched what remained of the baitfish, and the cameramen started upward with their underutilized gear. Running as low on air as everyone else, I prepared to follow the others up to the waiting *Nordon*. As I did so, I happened to glance over my right shoulder.

Directly behind me was a full-grown tiger shark. It was maybe a dozen feet away. It was also maybe a dozen feet long.

I would not be surprised if the bubble I released subsequent to encountering this wholly unexpected sight registered on seismic detection equipment hundreds of miles away in Perth. I might have verbalized something short and pungent—I honestly don't remember. Not that it would have mattered. Remember the advertising slogan for the classic science-fiction film *Alien*? To paraphrase it, underwater no one can hear you scream "Holy . . . !"

Whether it was the bubble, my sudden exclamation, the goggle-eyed look on my face, or the incredible velocity with which I began kicking backward, something startled the tiger. In a flash, it was gone; a blur of fins and teeth and tail. Collecting myself (just as on land, panic underwater uses air at an accelerated rate), I hovered there, up against the reef. The image of the tiger staring back at me remained imprinted on my retinas, like the colors you see when you squeeze your eyes very tightly shut.

For all I knew, the shark had been there the entire time, watching me watch the film crew watching Rodney. The perfect Gary Larson cartoon come to life.

Nobody else saw it. As soon as I made my turn and reacted, the shark took off. I'm not sure all of them believed me when, back on the boat, I related the story of my brief encounter. But some of them did. I think, for sure, Rodney did.

Maybe it was the look in my eyes.

VII

FLAT TIRES, OLD CANVAS, AND BIG CATS

Tanzania, July 1984

I COULD EASILY HAVE BEGUN this book with several stories about lions. When one thinks of predators, *Panthera leo* is often the first animal that comes to mind. Humans have been dealing with lions for a long time—usually to the lions' detriment—but our admiration for them has never flagged. There are heavier tigers, but little in nature is as impressive as a healthy male lion in full framing mane or a pride of sleek, muscular females focused on a hunt.

Years ago, my wife and I were fortunate to encounter the latter activity during a visit to Ngorongoro Crater National Park in Tanzania. Ignoring the flanking safari vehicles, the females were wholly intent on stalking a herd of placid wildebeests. As the pride members padded forward, eyes locked on their intended prey, they spread out in a horizontal line. Occasionally, each would pause to look down the line and check on the position of her sisters. In the end, the alerted wildebeests wandered out of easy hunting range and the lions, seemingly unperturbed by this development, nonchalantly settled down for an afternoon snooze. Those of us fortunate enough to have witnessed this demonstration of leonine tactics will never forget it.

Breaking off a stalk to take a nap is not unusual behavior for lions. They habitually sleep eighteen out of every twenty-four hours. This penchant for dozing can allow careful sightseers to approach a somnolent pride quite closely. Nothing looks more like a housecat than a female lion sleeping on her back, rear legs akimbo and moving lazily back and forth in her sleep while one front leg rests on her chest. It's the ultimate catnap.

The apparent lassitude is deceiving. Decades of acclimation to and acquaintance with tourist-packed safari 4x4s has led lions, with rare exceptions, to view driver, passengers, and vehicle as a whole. That's why during close approaches they may seem to ignore the car in which you are riding.

Step out of the car, however . . .

* * *

South Africa, May 2002

WHEN I WAS IN NAMIBIA in 1993, a deadly incident was reported over the wire services that originated from Kruger National Park in South Africa. Coming upon a pride of sleeping lions in the middle of the day, three male tourists from Taiwan got out of their car. (Kruger is liberally peppered with signs advising visitors in no-nonsense terms to STAY IN YOUR CAR.) Believing perhaps that Kruger operates as some sort of open-air subset of Disney World, two of them walked over to the slumbering group and turned around to have their photo taken with the picturesque pride. The lions, not unexpectedly, promptly woke up and ate them both. This outcome was shakily related to the press by the only survivor: the traumatized third visitor. Nominated by his friends to take the proposed picture, he had been close enough to the car to escape back into it. Once he was back inside the vehicle, the lions were no longer interested in him.

I had a chance to personally investigate this principle during my own exploration of Kruger. Though my visit took place years after the aforementioned incident, for all I know one of the same hulking felines that had exhibited a prior interest in Chinese food could have been the same one that ended up testing my friend and me.

Africa is home to many great national parks, from Ivindo and Loango in Gabon, to Etosha in Namibia, to the glorious but little-visited Ruaha in southwestern Tanzania. Along with the Serengeti, perhaps the most famous is Kruger. Previously the size of Switzerland, through the inclusion of congruent parks on its Zimbabwean and Mozambiquean borders, Kruger has been greatly expanded. Now known as the Great Limpopo Transfrontier Park, it is possibly the best place in all of Africa to easily see a vast variety of wildlife in a comparatively natural habitat.

I say easily because Kruger's immense size allows it to offer the visiting wildlife enthusiast a wide variety of inside-the-park accommodations. Good roads permit tourist buses to maintain regular sightseeing schedules. But if you really want to see Kruger, and spend some time listening to and observing wildlife as opposed to chattering primates from other countries, you need to get out on your own. Since for self-evident reasons setting out on a casual stroll through the park is absolutely forbidden (the rationale being one and the same with signs that say DON'T FEED THE ANIMALS), the best way to do this is to rent your own vehicle. While all visitors must be back in the numerous fenced camps by a specified early evening time, during the day you are free to drive where you will along the park's many miles of roads and linger wherever you wish.

I was traveling with a friend, the late fantasy artist Ron Walotsky. Ron had never been anywhere outside the States save for a brief trip to Europe. Kruger was our first stop after driving east from Johannesburg, and every bird, shrub, and creature we encountered was apt to elicit an excited request from him to stop the car so he could take pictures. I cheerfully obliged, keen to reacquaint myself with the marvels of the African bush.

We began our visit by staying two nights at Skukusa Rest Camp, the largest and most highly developed of the facilities inside the park. I have mentioned that every visitor and vehicle has to be back inside their respective camp boundaries by a designated time. The same strictures apply to departure. No one is allowed out of the camp until five-thirty in the morning. Hoping to be first out, vehicles start lining up in the dark around a quarter to five. We were sixth in line.

Two roads lead out of Skukusa: one that heads due south, where nursing hyenas had earlier been spotted, and the other east. A couple of miles outside the camp gate, a turnoff leads to a crossing of the Sabi River and shortly thereafter, to another that crosses the Sand River. Seeing that everyone else was staying on the main tracks, we opted for the lesser-used twin-river crossing. As soon as we made the necessary northward turn, we lost sight of any other vehicle. There was no car ahead of us and none behind. Nurtured by proximity to the two rivers, trees and brush closed in around us. I was driving.

Ten minutes out of camp, with Ron avidly studying the map of the park and riding copilot, I saw something on the road ahead. Gradually, our car drew a little closer. The dappled early morning light falling through the trees revealed the hind end of an animal and a long tail switching back and forth. Despite my rising sense of excitement, I looked at it for a long time before I felt confident in saying what I was thinking. There was a reason for this: I had been skunked before.

On my first trip to Amazonian Peru, I wanted more than anything else to see an anaconda. Motoring up the Manú River, I thought I spotted one, and excitedly yelled out, "Anaconda, anaconda!" while gesturing vigorously in the slender shape's direction. The boat driver quickly turned in the direction I was indicating, motoring slowly toward the left bank. It was soon apparent that my anaconda was nothing more than a twisted log bobbing against the riverbank. Thereafter, whenever we passed a suitably serpentine branch, either the guide or boatman would point and chortle loudly, "Anaconda!" It was a useful lesson. From then on, whenever and wherever I thought I had made an interesting animal "spot," I waited until I was sure of my identification.

So despite my initial disbelief at what I was seeing, this time I was sure.

Not in deep bush, not hiding among riverfront trees, but pacing methodically up the road ahead of us was a black leopard.

Still sleepy from rising early to park in line at the Skukusa gate,

PREDATORS I HAVE KNOWN

I blurted out to Ron, "I think that's a black leopard!" And then I just stared. Held the wheel and stared. Dimly, a voice at the back of my mind was screaming in a desperate attempt to get my attention. "Camera! Get the *camera*!"

Eventually, the notion drifted to the forefront of my stunned mind, and I finally began fumbling with my gear. By the time I had the battery mounted and the camera turned on, the leopard had cast a single contemptuous glance in our direction, turned sharply to its left, and disappeared into the undergrowth. We drew up alongside the place where it had entered the brush. There was no sign it had ever existed. One of the rarest sightings I have ever experienced, and I was late with the camera again. This is why professional photographers *always* have a camera loaded, ready, activated, and at hand, and battery conservation be damned. In my personal litany of missed shots, the black leopard of Kruger ranks right up there with the Kanha tiger looking down at me from atop the dry riverbank.

On our third night, we transferred our base of operations to Olifants Rest Camp. Located much deeper inside the park than Skukusa, Olifants is too far away to be reached by day-trippers. Perched atop a high bluff overlooking the Olifants River (where did you think Tolkien got the name?), the individual *bomas* (round cabins built in traditional local style) were charming and comfortable. We relaxed, Ron sketching the landscape with his portable artist's watercolor set, and determined to pursue our routine of being up and about out as early as possible the next morning.

Retracing our route along Kruger's main north-south road the following day, we encountered a quartet of trotting rhinos, a second (normal-hued) leopard, and the usual cornucopia of wildlife for which Kruger is justly famous. Parked before a small pond, we watched as zebras and giraffes arrived to drink their morning fill.

It was south of the Ngotso Weir waterhole that we were forced to slow when we unexpectedly found the road ahead blocked by half a dozen parked cars. None of them were tour buses or park vehicles. All were private transport like our own. Seeing that everyone was looking in the same direction, we turned our attention toward the source of all the interest. It didn't take much searching to locate it.

A pride had made an impala kill close to the road and was tearing into the morning meal with typical predatory gusto. Deep-throated roars and domineering growls filled the air. One by one, too soon jaded by the sight or too locked into a predetermined travel schedule, the other vehicles moved off and continued on their way. Eventually, only ours and one other car were left.

A male lion attempted to approach the carcass, on which a pair of cubs was now feeding. Their mother drove him off with a furious charge, ferocious snarl, and flurry of flailing paws that set the male up on his hind legs and would have had any professional wildlife documentarian's camera running full-out. I managed to record a little of the explosive action, albeit while having to shoot over Ron's shoulder. When things settled down again, the other remaining car started up and came toward us. Stopping on my side, the driver rolled his window down halfway, nodded toward the front of our vehicle, and spoke with some concern in his voice.

"Say, did you know that your front left tire is completely flat?"

My mind still reeling from the image of charging female lion and towering male, I digested this information blankly. While commendably pithy, I'm afraid my polite response to our fellow traveler's query fell somewhat short of memorable.

"Really?" I mumbled.

The man nodded, his expression somber. "Completely flat."

I looked at Ron. Ron looked at me. I looked back at the helpful visitor in the other car. The nearest help was at Timbavati Camp, ten miles away. Our concerned fellow travelers were not going that direction. They were headed due south and had a schedule to keep. What to do?

"Listen," I told him, "when you get to Satara, would you tell them that they've got a vehicle stuck up here?"

"Sure." The man hesitated. "Are you going to be OK?"

I nodded, secure in knowledge I didn't possess. "We've got plenty of water and food. We'll be all right."

The visitor and his friends drove off, heading south. I could only hope that they would be as good as their word to report our situation.

We did have ample water, and snacks. Something else we had in plenty, and what I had not considered when assuring the other visitors that we would be fine, was the heat. As the day wore on, the tropical sun rose steadily higher in the sky. The hours passed and our car's interior periodically grew unbearably hot. I say periodically because from time to time we would fire up the engine so we could run the air-conditioning. Of course, as soon as we turned it off, it took about two minutes for the interior to become stifling all over again, whereupon we had the choice of opening the windows or suffocating.

Meanwhile, off in the tawny high grass to the right and just in front of us, the remaining lions were quietly polishing off the last of the impala carcass.

Maybe, I thought, *the man had been hasty in his appraisal of our condition. He had spoken with an accent. Perhaps where he came from even a slightly flat tire counted as completely flat. Could he have been mistaken? Were we sitting there baking in the African sun for no good reason?* There was just one problem with this encouraging possibility.

How to find out.

I turned to Ron. "Watch the lions."

He looked back at me. "I am watching the lions."

"No," I corrected him, "I mean keep an eye on them. I'm going to check the tire."

He stared. "O-o-o-o-h . . . k-a-a-a-y," he said finally.

The road offered a certain amount of open space. At least, out on the pavement, nothing could sneak up on me. The remnants of the pride were a good thirty yards away and busily occupied. I tried to tell myself they would stay that way. Opening the door as quietly as I could, I gingerly put first one foot on the asphalt, then the other, careful to make no noise. Emerging from the car and straightening, my eyes were in constant motion as I tried to inspect the front end while simultaneously keeping watch on the tall grass on the other side of the vehicle. Needless to say, my inspection was a quick one.

Sliding as quickly as possible back into the car, I looked at Ron.

"Well?" he asked me.

"You never saw such a flat tire."

"Then we're still stuck."

My reply was uncharitable. "Unless you want to get out and change the tire," I said helpfully. "I'm sure there's a spare and a jack in the back."

He had turned back in the direction of the feeding pride. "Umm . . . no, I don't think so."

Another hour passed without any sign of an approaching vehicle, much less a tow truck or repair van. We were alone. The sun continued to rise. By my casual estimation, it was now at least 150 degrees outside the car and 200 or 300 within. The road in front of us stayed empty, as did the road behind us. How long would it take for our fellow travelers to reach Satara, inform someone in a position of responsibility of our predicament, have someone in authority authorize a tow truck or other service vehicle to start our way, and actually get here? Assuming any of that transpired, of course, and that the other travelers had not forgotten about us completely.

I pictured our erstwhile saviors sitting in the café at Satara discussing their day's adventures and sipping cold drinks. I pictured the little streams of condensation running down the sides of their ice-cold bottles of beer or soda. I pictured . . .

Ron was suddenly sitting forward and gesturing excitedly. "The lion, the lion!"

What lion? I thought. Oh, he must mean the one that's walking straight toward us. *That* lion.

Expressive of mane, mouth open, tongue lolling, and weighing between 400 and 500 pounds, the pride's dominant male had come out of the grass and was ambling coolly across the road toward our stranded vehicle. I hastily recalled everything I had ever read about lions regarding people inside cars as being part of the car. I strove mightily to generate around myself a dense air of inedibility. I also remembered that my window was completely rolled down. Our rental had power windows.

I stared at the oncoming big cat the way one does at other awe-inspiring

natural phenomena like tornados or tidal waves: momentarily too paralyzed by the overwhelming sight to move. Beside me, Ron was hissing
tersely.

"Get the picture. Get the picture!"

That moved me to action. "Get the *picture*? The hell with the picture! *You* get the picture!" The lion was very close now. Much too close,
approaching the front bumper on my side of the car. As I reached for the
button to raise my window, I remembered that the engine was off. The
window stayed down. Frantically, I began fumbling with the key in the
ignition. I couldn't find the position on the rented car's steering column
that would allow me to activate its accessories. I pushed the key hard
over. The engine refused to start.

I began to panic. *I was part of the car*, I told myself. There was nothing to worry about. Unless this particular lion was unaware of that bit
of information. Spread wide, his paw would be large enough to cover my
entire face. Or remove it. I struggled with the key, trying to watch it and
the lion at once. If I put too much pressure on the key and broke it, or
jammed it in the ignition . . .

I looked again to my right. The lion's mouth, which at the now greatly
reduced distance between us was as big as the mouth of a trash can
and just as commodious, had drawn parallel to the car's radio antenna.
Something inside the steering column clicked softly. Whirling, I jabbed a
finger at the button mounted on the armrest. Much too slowly, the window started up. As it was rising, the lion, attracted either by the noise
or by the movement inside the car, turned his head in my direction. His
eyes passed over me and for just an instant, met mine. I froze. All he had
to do was reach up, stick a paw inside the car, and fish out the paralyzed
food trapped inside. Dropping his eyes, he turned back to the pavement
in front of him and continued on without pausing next to the car. I was
just another component of the peculiar unchewable object on wheels and
therefore of no interest. Or maybe he was not interested because he had
just eaten.

Since I was already sweating about as profusely as possible from
the heat, I can't say that I noticed much difference in the amount of

perspiration trickling down my body. But it would have been interesting at that moment to have taken my pulse. Had the window remained wide open and the lion been disinclined to conform to standard lion practice, I would not be recalling the close confrontation now. I would have joined the unfortunate impala on the afternoon's buffet. My breathing eased as I watched the big cat recede behind the car.

"Did you get the picture?" I finally asked Ron.

"Picture?" He looked at me sheepishly. "No, I was too busy watching."

I stared at Ron for a long moment. My fingers may have twitched. Then I turned the key fully in the ignition. I'd had enough of baking in the sun and playing potentially fatal peekaboo with hungry apex predators.

Driving at a consistent speed of precisely three miles per hour, we eventually succeeded in limping into Timbavati. There, a curious mechanic contemplated our completely flat front tire, eyed me disapprovingly, and asked, "Why didn't you just change it?"

I don't remember my exact reply, but I do recall that I managed to respond in words of more than four letters.

* * *

Tanzania, August 1984

AS TANZANIA'S FIRST PRESIDENT, JULIUS Nyerere was admired by many, both inside Africa and out. Opinions regarding the rest of his government and many of his policies tended to be considerably less complimentary. Under the communist-socialist system he imposed, the usual inescapable afflictions of state-run commerce affected every aspect of Tanzanian society. Shortages of basics became even more commonplace than elsewhere in East Africa, industry stumbled along deprived of raw materials, and traditional African subsistence agriculture found itself subsumed into the familiar dreary people's communes where no one is inspired to work one iota harder than they absolutely must to avoid the approbation of their fellows.

For years, a reader of mine named Bill Smythe had been imploring my wife and me to visit him and his wife, Sally, in Tanzania. Bill was a rodent control expert who had worked for various international aid programs everywhere from Fiji to Pakistan to Somalia and was, at that time, posted to Morogoro, a medium-size city about three hours' drive inland from Tanzania's capital of Dar es Salaam.

"Come on over," he kept writing. "I'll save up our gas ration coupons, and we'll take a couple of drives around the country."

This invitation finally being too tempting to ignore, JoAnn and I eventually found ourselves on a British Airways flight from London to Dar, with brief layovers in Cairo and Khartoum. As a harbinger of interesting developments to come, even these two brief stops proved themselves of interest.

Assigned to the forward section of the plane, we turned in our seats as in Cairo group after group of white-clad men and women boarded the aircraft. A number of the men sported ritual scars on their cheeks. Noting our curious stares, one of the crew proceeded to enlighten us.

"They all live in Khartoum. This is their shopping flight. There's nothing to buy in Khartoum, so they take this middle portion of the flight back and forth to do their shopping in Cairo."

Sure enough, when we arrived in Khartoum and parked on the tarmac, every one of the passengers who had boarded in Cairo promptly got off. As the last of them deplaned and the aircraft sat, I was able to steal a look out the door. No terminal was visible. In the warm desert night, the lights of the capitol of Sudan glistened in the distance. Driven by a steady breeze, swirls and whorls of sand danced across the runway while a pair of guards armed with AK-47s stood guard on either side of the rolling stairway. At any moment, I expected Sydney Greenstreet to arrive in a jeep and make a mad dash for the plane with an agitated Peter Lorre in tow.

Bathed in sunshine and carpeted with flowers, Morogoro sits at the foot of the imposing Uluguru Mountains. For days, we enjoyed Bill and Sally's hospitality (Sally's chicken-fried warthog is to die for . . . perhaps I should rephrase that: It's wonderfully good), traveling to little-visited spots like Ruaha National Park. The finale of our visit was to consist of a long drive northward, in the course of which, we would visit several better-known national parks. At its conclusion, our hosts, unable to legally cross into Kenya with their little Subaru wagon, would drop us at the customs and immigration station at the border. There, we could walk across the dividing line and on the other side hire a taxi to take us to Nairobi.

Our first stop was Lake Manyara National Park, full of hippos, herds of antelope of several species, and the oldest elephant I have ever seen. Our next was Tarangire National Park.

Like every other business in Tanzania, the tourist industry had taken a huge hit thanks to the communist government's inherent ineptness. Over the years, word of chronic shortages and mismanagement had driven away all but the most determined and dedicated visitors. In the course of our travels, we experienced firsthand just what a central bureaucracy can do to a previously thriving business.

For example, in the formerly excellent hotels where we stayed, lightbulbs were nowhere to be found. Staff had purloined every one of them for personal use or resale. This proved to be true of many hotel basics, from toilet paper to towels. At the spectacularly sited hotel on the rim of Ngorongoro Crater, we had to pass a small bribe to one of the staff to get an extra blanket. This was necessary so we wouldn't freeze to death during the night because the hotel had no heat. Repeated attempts to order off elaborate dining room menus invariably met politely apologetic replies of, "I'm sorry, sir, but that selection is currently unavailable." We learned quickly enough that instead of wasting time participating in this charade, it was much quicker and easier to simply ask which one of the sixty-three listed choices the kitchen actually did have on hand that day, and be satisfied with that. Compared to trying to identify an edible entrée, dessert was a simple matter. We ate more canned fruit salad than we ever had before or since.

At the Mount Meru Hotel in Arusha, the center of northern Tanzania's tourist trade, we encountered something that to this day remains utterly unique in all my travels. Turning on the hot water tap in the bathtub brought forth an immediate gush of steaming hot water. Attempting to moderate it by turning on the cold water tap produced a furious stream of . . . steaming hot water. The same was true of the water that flowed from both sink faucets.

Talk about your surreal travel experience. A hotel bathroom that serves up only *hot* water.

The rolling hills and plentiful wildlife of Tarangire were rendered all the more stunning and memorable by the fact that the four of us were the only visitors. Having the park to ourselves made us feel as if we had taken a step back in time, to when visits to Africa were the sole province of the very rich or the very daring.

As it developed, the last half of that description fit our accommodations perfectly.

Bill had told us prior to our arrival that Tarangire, being less developed as well as less famous than the Serengeti or Ngorongoro, was a tented camp. Exactly what this meant was not spelled out. I'm not sure Bill knew all the details himself. But we quickly learned them. There were twelve big tents, arranged in a straight line facing distant hills.

Ours was large if not spacious, with a ceiling high enough to allow us to move around inside without having to bend. Furnishings consisted of a small table on which was placed a pitcher of (hopefully) boiled water and a glass (that had hopefully been cleaned in boiling water). There was a small camp chair and, aligned on opposite sides of the tent and about six feet from each other, two individual cots with bedding. A kerosene lantern hung from the tent's apex. The dull green canvas walls reflected a lack of maintenance sufficient to suggest that nothing like a preservative or cleaning compound had come in contact with the aged material since the British had abandoned East Africa to the locals back in the 1950s. In places, the primitive, heavy fabric was torn or peeling. Out the tent's back entrance was a portable toilet that was open to the sky and enclosed on three sides by wooden slats.

My wife, who is less than fond of camping, surveyed our other-than-five-star accommodations.

"It'll be all right," I told her. "It's only for two nights."

She nodded . . . dubiously.

Given the option of staying in any of the vacant tents, Bill and Sally had understandably chosen one several sites away from ours. As we settled in for the night, the temperature remained pleasant while the air retained the freshness of the day but without the exacerbating heat. Having turned out the lantern, I used my small flashlight to find my cot and slip beneath the more-or-less clean blanket and single sheet.

"Good night, hon."

"Good night," she replied tiredly.

Some two minutes later, a sound reverberated through the tent's interior. It was a long, low baying, the kind a vigorous steer might make after undertaking six months' opera training in Milan. A single extended bellow followed by a series of shorter coughs. It wasn't unimpressive.

Nor did it escape JoAnn's notice. Any hint of the fatigue incurred as a consequence of the day's long drive vanished from her voice.

"What was that?"

I did my best to sound blasé. "The lions."

Her response emphasized each word carefully. "*What* 'lions'?"

"Just 'the lions,'" I replied diffidently. I tried to will myself instantly to sleep. It did not work.

I could hear her moving around and sitting up on the other cot. "There are lions here? How close are they?" As if responding to a cue card, another of the large unseen felines promptly embarked upon an imposing extended bawl. As soon as he or she stopped, the cry was taken up by another, and then another. The bellowing was now coming from multiple directions and no doubt from different prides. From a traditional choral standpoint their liturgy was limited, but no less impressive for the lack of Latin.

"Not too close," I offered, more out of hope than knowledge.

JoAnn bought that about as much as she accepted that I had suddenly become fluent in Swahili. "How do *you* know? How can you tell? How *close* are they?"

I tried another tack. "We're fine. They won't bother us in here."

Her flashlight winked on. A bad sign. She played it over the interior walls of the tent, pausing briefly to isolate a gigantic Jerusalem cricket that was ascending the back wall. "What do you mean, 'we're fine'?

Don't you see this canvas? It's all rotten! A lion could get in here with one swipe!"

"Maybe one could," I argued weakly, "but they won't."

"Oh no? How do *you* know that?"

"I just," I sputtered, "I mean, they *don't*, that's all." All else having failed, I fell to resorting to logic. "If they did, nobody would rent these tents."

"That's not a good enough reason." The light moved, and I felt her presence against me. "Move over. I'm sleeping with you tonight."

I tried to make room and quickly found myself lying across the cot's less than forgiving outside support pole. It was patently obvious that it was not the intention of the cot's designers that someone should sleep half in and half out of their product. I so informed JoAnn.

"Neither one of us will get any sleep this way," I pleaded.

"Fine! Then neither one of us will get any sleep. You're on the outside. If they come through that wall, they'll eat you first."

And thus was established our routine for the rest of the night. Every time exhaustion grew so complete and overwhelming that I thought I might actually drift off to sleep, another lion would verbally assail the moon, or call to a mate, or exercise its lungs just for the leonine hell of it. Whereupon a freshly wide-awake JoAnn would give me a sharp nudge and declare insistently, "That was close, wasn't it? How close was that?"

Four new *bomas* were under construction at the campsite—meaning they had not been touched in weeks. Thus far, each consisted of four walls fashioned of rough concrete blocks, a bare concrete floor, a couple of windows, a front door, and a metal roof. The second night at Tarangire that was where we slept—on the floor. And the most delicious part of our visit?

In all the time we spent roaming Tarangire, we did not see a single lion.

* * *

Mount Etjo, Namibia, October 1993

FELIX THE CHEETAH WAS THE only semi-wild animal at Mount Etjo, but he was far from the only big cat. The extensive Okonjati Wildlife Sanctuary was home to caracal, leopard, and, of course, lion. To ensure that visitors had the opportunity to see lions feeding, from time to time, a haunch of antelope or whatever meat was available would be set out. Such a procedure is not uncommon at private game reserves. What makes it special at Okonjati is that the feeding is done at night, when big predators tend to be more active, and that viewing is done not from the safety of a big Land Rover or Unimog, but from ground level.

Below ground level, actually.

A long approach ditch had been dug and covered with cut brush, and at the end of it is a transverse ditch like the cap of the letter "T," which has also been covered and camouflaged. I'd seen such blinds before, but they had been built to allow quiet viewing of birds or herbivores. Not nocturnally feeding lions. When the setup was being explained to the visitors at the lodge, one gentleman from Germany raised a hand to inquire, reasonably, as to what was there to keep the lions from adding observing humans to the evening menu.

"They have the meat that's been set out for them," the guide explained. "Also, there's an electrically charged wire running in front of the blind."

"One wire?" the German gentleman asked.

The guide nodded. "One's enough. They know not to try and cross it."

To me this sounded not unlike the other guide's remark about not knowing cheetahs didn't like to be scratched between their front legs.

"Nobody's been attacked while watching the feed," the guide added. Seeing that some of the visitors were wavering, he did not add "yet."

It was very dark. Little moonlight. Those of us who decided to go were bussed out into the bush and then escorted down the trench that had been dug to provide access to the main blind. No one asked if there was anything to prevent a curious lion from entering via the same artificial gully.

Once at the blind, we spread out. A couple of spotlights illuminated a chunk of dead meat from which protruded a single leg. In the reduced light, I couldn't tell what ungulate it was from, but it was considerably bigger than an impala. The smell emanating from the carcass was profound. We didn't have to wait long.

Huffing and growling, the pride came in at a quick jog. If they sensed our presence they gave no sign of it. Their attention was concentrated wholly on food that wasn't going to run away. Females began to rip off big pieces of flesh and carry them off into the darkness beyond the reach of the spotlights while adolescents hung around the fringe waiting for a chance at the carcass. Then the males arrived. Awkwardly, from the perspective of the lionesses, there were two of them, and they both promptly laid claim to the biggest hunk of meat. One on each side, both dug in with teeth and claws. Neither was willing to give way. Back and forth, they wrestled, pushed, shoved, ignoring the staring humans in the ditch as each sought to assert its dominance over the other.

The problem was that in their single-minded attempt to gain control of the free meal, they kept edging closer and closer to the blind.

I didn't know how much voltage was flowing through the single wire that was both our defensive moat and palisade. But, at that moment, it looked about as effective as a cable downloading music to an iPod. One of the Italians nervously asked the guard if maybe we should call it a night. The guide shook his head no and put a finger to his lips.

Whether it was the presence of the electrified wire or simply fatigue, the two males halted inches from the inadequate barrier. Neither had relinquished his grip on the meat. They were, I estimated, no more than six or seven feet away. I could have stretched out flat on the ground, stuck a hand beneath the wire, and made contact with my toes still hanging over the edge of the ditch. It was plain they weren't at all interested in us, however. What rendered the situation intimidating was not so much their proximity as the fact that crouching in the blind we were at eye level with them. Seeing a lion at eye level is very different from observing one from the back of a truck or other 4x4. Their mass becomes overwhelming, the definition in the straining muscles awe-inspiring.

Having settled into their tug-of-war, both males had gone comparatively quiet as well as motionless. We began to relax a little. It was plain that sooner or later one male would take control of the meat and walk off into the night with it, just as the females had done earlier. I found myself blinking. It had been a long, hot day. After witnessing the feeding, it would be good to get back to the room, lie down, and relax. Except for a few insects, there was little noise now and . . .

The lions exploded.

I don't know how else to describe it. For nearly ten minutes, they had been staring at each other, their faces a couple of feet apart, virtually silent as each strained to take control of the evening meal from his brother when, without warning, they erupted in a sequence of roars, slaps, and violent contortions that were powerful enough to, as the learned sages used to say, freeze the blood.

As quickly as the eruption had taken place, it quieted.

One of the women had started to scream, and it had caught in her throat—a sound nearly as extraordinary as the one made by the two lions. Everyone, including me, had momentarily jerked slightly backward. Time, existence, the air . . . had for an instant been stopped. Then the lion brothers resumed their silent contest of strength and will, and a number of human bodies resumed their normal patterns of respiration. It was one of the most extraordinary couple of seconds I have ever experienced, vastly heightened by the fact that it occurred only a few feet in front of me.

Ever since, I have not been able to look at a lion, no matter how quiescent, or sleepy, or indifferent, or far away behind moat or bars in a zoo, in the same way again.

VIII

MEANWHILE, SAFELY BACK HOME...

Prescott, Arizona, Anytime

FRIENDS I MAKE IN REMOTE locales overseas or meet on the trail are wont to assume that the carnivores with whom I have encounters are only to be found in the exotic far-flung corners of the earth: in the searing deserts of Africa and the steaming jungles of Asia, South America, and India. They are wrong. My home state of Arizona is full of hungry predators, some of whom are not even connected with the chief political parties. A sampling of such creatures can even be found in the primary urban areas of Phoenix and Tucson.

Though it continues to grow by demographic leaps and geriatric bounds (Prescott is always rated one of the best places in the United States to retire), the town where I live is still in many aspects quite rural. Much of this is due to the fact that on two sides the city limits back up against protected national forest. While the chances of having a black bear stumble into town, as used to happen every once in a while years ago, is now greatly reduced, the occasional curious cougar still pads its stealthy way into the outer fringes of development, no doubt hoping to chance upon a plump poodle or overly emboldened Chihuahua that has unadvisedly wandered away from its cosseted home base.

A live creek runs through our property, and while we have yet to encounter a cougar, the permanent water source draws a considerable variety of wildlife to its easily accessible banks. Predator-wise, I've seen both bobcats and foxes on our property. Nothing clears the sleep from your eyes immediately upon climbing out of bed than opening your curtains to find a fox glaring directly back at you, furious that your actions have startled the ground squirrel it has been patiently stalking among the rocks.

Most prominent and in many ways the most charismatic of the local predators is the coyote, *Canis latrans*. Not, as Chuck Jones would have it, *Eatanythingus gluttonus*. So clever and adaptable has the coyote proven to be that it can now be found almost everywhere in the United States, including within heavily developed city boundaries. So well has it done that it has come to be regarded as a "problem" animal worthy of serious control efforts, especially in urban terrain like Southern California that favors its efforts at concealment.

We don't have quite the same predicament in Arizona, because the coyotes here are not especially interested in concealing themselves. In their never-ending search for prey, they wander at will through the largest cities. Drainage washes and arroyos serve as their highways. While rodents and other small mammals are their preferred quarry, a hungry coyote will eat almost anything. Even a roadrunner, except that this famous member of the cuckoo family is not only hard to catch but compared to other prey is tough, sinewy, and not much of a meal for a large canid.

While coyotes most assuredly will take small pets that accidentally cross their path, like any predator, they prefer their natural prey. Often depicted in film and cartoons as stringy and emaciated, in reality, most coyotes are relatively robust animals. Around my hometown, some have bulked up to positively lupine proportions. Between the locally exploding ground squirrel and rabbit populations, they no longer even have to hunt. They just stand in the middle of the road and let addled hyperactive rabbits run into them.

I once drove the last few yards leading up to our gate only to come upon an enormous coyote standing squarely athwart the dirt road. Unable to drive around it, I slowed and came to a complete stop. It turned, regally, to gaze at me, utterly unmoved either by my direct human stare or the vehicle I was driving. This confrontation continued for some time; the coyote in no hurry to move, I thoroughly enjoying the moment—and not only because relating this anecdote gives me the rare opportunity to use the word *athwart.*

Eventually tiring of the encounter, I honked the horn. The coyote didn't move. Leaning out the window, I yelled at the creature. It blinked and looked toward the nearby creek. I let loose with a series of rising yips that I hoped might convey in approximated coyote language both my indignation and impatience. It looked back at me as if to say that one of us was an idiot, and it wasn't the one who was commuting on four legs.

Finally, after I had shut up and when the coyote was at last good and ready, it loped off into the brush. There it paused to watch me as I drove on past. Clearly, it was deep in coyote thought. Sometimes I wish I knew what it had been thinking. Other times, I'm glad I do not. I have a suspicion I would not have come off well.

Anyone who doubts the fabled intelligence of coyotes has never seen them work a dog. A pack will send one of their number out to irritate, play with, engage, do everything but seduce the subject of the group's interest. The appropriately star-struck dog will then chase, accompany, attempt to mate with, or for whatever reason of its own follow the solitary coyote away from the doghouse and into the bush. Whereupon the pack will reveal its true intent in luring the domesticated pooch away from the safety of its human domicile, said objective being to invite the clueless animal to dinner, with dog to be the main course.

But when visitors to Arizona and the American Southwest think of dangerous local carnivores, the rattlesnake is the creature far more likely to spring to mind than the coyote. Once again, we have to recognize the fact that as humans we are more visually than intellectually oriented. While the coyote's stealth, ability to hunt in packs, natural cunning, size, and penchant for picking off household pets make it the far more dangerous predator, its resemblance to human's best friend, its warm-bloodedness, and the fact that its natural ferocity has been disarmed by decades of appearances as a hapless cartoon character mean that the poor rattler is the one that consistently suffers from a bad press.

Whereas a hungry coyote is a threat to anything it is capable of carrying off, even a starving rattlesnake would rather slither away than bite. Despite their far greater numbers, the few serious encounters that take place each year between humans and rattlers can invariably be attributed to accident or stupidity (human stupidity, the snake invariably grading out higher on the intelligence scale when the particulars of such encounters are closely examined).

All rattlers are poisonous, the most dangerous being the green, or Mojave, rattlesnake. You would think this widely known fact would be sufficient, at least in Arizona, to discourage humans from initiating contact with them. Yet visitors to the desert and mountains, who by their very existence set new standards for redefining the word *fool*, persist in trying to pick them up by their tails, deliberately annoy them by throwing objects at them to make them rattle, or in dim-witted displays of misplaced machismo taunt them while at the same time seeing how close they can dance without being bitten. Try any of that with your average five-year-old and you're likely to get bit, too.

Though we live in prime rattlesnake territory, over the decades, we have had very few encounters with them. Despite what you tend to see in film and on television, rattlesnakes actually prefer not to bite. It takes food and energy and time to manufacture venom—venom that is more efficaciously employed in catching food. If you should happen to come across a rattler, slowly back away from it, turn around, and leave the area as quickly as you can. Both you and the snake will be happy that you did. Almost all rattlesnake bites are accidents resulting from hikers not seeing the snake. Step on any animal, however inadvertently, and it is guaranteed to bite.

Of course, when you come home one day with an armful of groceries and there's a rattler as big around as your arm lying on the flagstone directly in front of your front door, you are confronted with a conundrum that cannot be so easily avoided. It's a situation your typical urban dweller never has to face.

As it happened, I didn't have to face it, either.

My wife was returning home with a couple of male friends of ours. Before she could intervene or even be made aware of the snake's presence, they had killed it with rocks. Deciding that they would have a good giggle at her expense, as she returned to the front door to let them in, they confronted her with the dead snake, waving it up and down while uttering what they presumed to be scary noises.

My wife hails from west-central Texas. If you grow up in the country in west-central Texas, every time you step out your front door, you are as likely to encounter a rattlesnake as you are a neighbor. Raised with this likelihood in mind, children in that part of the world grow up knowing how to deal with every possible serpentine scenario. Contemplating the recently demised reptile, JoAnn evaluated it for a moment before saying, "Give it to me."

Exchanging a suddenly uncertain glance, our friends complied. My wife studied the dead snake briefly before gripping it firmly at the front end. Using both hands, she then proceeded to skin it, starting at the head and working progressively downward. Both friends suddenly found themselves on the opposite side of their intended gross-out prank.

Unfortunately, JoAnn did not have time to cure the skin properly. It would have made a nice hatband, if not a belt. I was out of town and didn't have a chance to see it. I relate this tale as a caution to any would-be burglars. I live with a woman who is part Cherokee, part Comanche, skins rattlesnakes with her bare hands, and carries a titanium switchblade.

The weaker sex, indeed.

* * *

As I mentioned earlier, we all have our specific, individual fears. JoAnn has no trouble dealing with a dead rattlesnake, and because of her upbringing she was sternly taught, and quite rightly so, to beware of live ones. She does not much care for sharks, although the likelihood of encountering a great white in the lakes bordering Prescott is pretty slim. She is also, like most folks, something of an arachnophobe. Myself,

I hold the same kind of soft spot for spiders that I do for all the underdog species that frequently appear in the garish headlines of our tabloid media.

Which is a roundabout way of segueing to the day JoAnn came home to find me making friends with a tarantula.

Of all Arizona's native predators, none has a more undeserved reputation for posing a danger to humans than the poor slandered representatives of the family *Theraphosidae.* Certainly tarantulas will bite if sufficiently provoked (so will an irritated five-year-old). But by and large, they are among the most serene of spiders. They cannot help how they look, nor the fact that other, smaller relatives like the black widow and the brown recluse really are dangerous. Remember what I said before: It's always the smaller things that get you.

It was one of those early summer chamber-of-commerce days in Prescott. In the mountains of central Arizona, assorted migratory species such as hummingbirds, deer, and tourists were on the march. So, too, was the tarantula that ambled toward me as I was standing outside our front door gazing down at the creek that flows past our house. As representatives of its kind go, it was not particularly large. Nothing like the Goliath spiders of the Amazon, whose bodies are bigger than a man's spread hand and whose outstretched legs would fit comfortably over the top of a basketball. This fuzzy eight-legged visitor could have nestled comfortably in my open palm. In the bright sunlight, I could see its twin fangs plainly, glistening as if whittled from black ivory.

I realize that this image is by itself enough to acutely unsettle the arachnophobes among you. Please be at your ease. I am not about to be bitten and run screaming, and neither are you. Think, if you must envision something spidery, of *Charlotte's Web.*

The road to our property either dead-ends against our driveway or becomes our driveway, depending on how much sightseeing someone careening along it happens to be doing. As the road merges into our driveway, dirt gives way to gravel. The house itself sits on a level terrace between two sharply sloping hillsides. The downslope below the house gives way to some landscaped Arizona cypress, vinca ground cover, outcroppings of pale yellow and tan granitic rock, and below that, the creek. My study is in a room located above a detached garage.

The tarantula was in the process of migrating, or so I guessed taking into consideration the temperature, humidity, and time of year. (Unlike Wile E. Coyote might have done, it was not holding up a neatly lettered little sign reading I AM MIGRATING.) Having probably made its way upward from somewhere near the creek and then navigated through the ground-level jungle of dark-green vinca, the tarantula emerged daintily out into the sunlight and commenced a straightforward traverse of the gravel driveway.

The afternoon was warm and cloudless. I was returning to the house from the study when I saw it. I paused for a couple of moments to monitor its progress, noting the flawless combination of grace and agility with which it was making its sure-footed way across the wide, dry, rocky expanse. On impulse, out of curiosity, and having nothing else to do for the immediate moment, I sat down deliberately in its path.

While I had spent a good deal of time around its kind previously, both in zoos and in the jungle, I had never before been so bold as to attempt to make physical contact. I figured the right moment had come. After all, the tarantula was on my property. Could I do less than extend a sociable greeting?

Encountering my fully extended left leg slightly above the knee, it paused. One hairy black leg, then a second, commenced to inspect this sudden obstacle. Would it go around? It would not. Maintaining the same measured pace, it proceeded to climb up my leg and over the top. Through the fabric of the jeans I was wearing, I could clearly feel its weight and its movements. Living as most of us do in temperate or cold climates, the insects and arachnids we happen upon are usually modest in size. We tend not to think of them as having much in the way of mass or weight. My visitor had both.

As the tarantula rappeled down the inside of my thigh, crossed a narrow strip of gravel, and started up my right leg, my wife drove up and parked nearby. Wishing to know what I was doing sitting out in the sun in the middle of the driveway, she exited the car and came around the front. Well, partway around the front. She halted as soon as she saw the multilegged dark shape that was in the process of traversing my right leg. Her tone was very deliberate.

"What . . . are . . . you . . . *doing?*"

I gestured at my new acquaintance. "Isn't it beautiful?"

"No," my wife snapped. "It's not. Are you crazy? What if it bites you?"

"It won't bite me." I was very sure of myself.

"How do you know?"

"Because it's already been over one leg, and it didn't bite me." I beckoned. "Come have a look."

JoAnn started forward—in the direction of the front door. "Do whatever you want with it, but I don't want that thing anywhere *near* the house."

"Relax." I smiled reassuringly. "It's just crossing the driveway." I gestured to my right. "In a couple of minutes, it'll be up in the spruce bushes on the other side and you'll never see it again."

"Good!" The front door closed behind my wife.

I was tempted to find a way to prolong the dalliance, but I had no desire to unnecessarily tire my mellow caller or inhibit its migration. And besides, it was hot sitting in the sun. As soon as the tarantula had finished its transect of the author, I rose. Perhaps my shadow startled it. In any event, it picked up its pace noticeably. I watched until it did indeed disappear into the rocks and bushes that formed a wall on the far side of the driveway, whereupon I returned to my study and my work and thought no more of it.

The following afternoon, not long after lunch, the phone on my desk rang. The voice on the other end was immediately recognizable as well as uncharacteristically agitated.

"Get down here. *Right now.*"

JoAnn's words alarmed me. "Why? What's wrong?"

Her tone turned taut. "Your *friend* is in the house."

"My . . . ?" It took a moment before realization dawned. "That's impossible. With the air-conditioning on, everything's closed up, and it's too big to get under the screen doors."

"Maybe it used the handle. It's big enough for *that*." My wife's words were joking but her tone was not. "Get down here *this minute* and get that tarantula *out of my house*."

"It won't hurt you." My guarantee fell on deaf ears. Or rather, on no ears. JoAnn had hung up.

The tarantula was in the kitchen, feeling its way methodically along the base of the cabinets, probing for suitable openings. Unlike other youthful visitors to our home, I knew it was looking for a cricket, not a cookie. "The tarantula in the kitchen," I murmured to my wife. "Nice title for a story."

"How about 'dead tarantula in the kitchen'?" JoAnn glared at me. "It's your friend. *You* get it out. Or I'm getting a shoe." Her nervous gaze returned to the spider, which was attempting to find a way into the space beneath the sink. "Make that a boot. A big boot."

"Calm down. I'll get it out."

All it took was a large jar and a piece of cardboard. Eye to eyes, I studied the tarantula up close as its front legs pawed at the inside of the glass.

"Naughty, naughty," I told it. "You need to learn to knock." I looked over at JoAnn. "Look at it this way: You didn't find the tarantula in bed."

My wife stared back at me. "If I ever find that thing in bed with me, there are gonna be *two* dead bodies to throw out."

I placed our intruder in the car and took it far, far away. To the shore of Willow Lake, where I released it into a field of dense grass doubtless gravid with grasshoppers and other suitable chitonous prey. I watched until the tarantula had disappeared from view and hoped it would find an accommodating abandoned burrow in which to spend the night. In the course of our brief encounters, it had neither nipped me nor flung a defensive cloudlet of its kind's urticating hairs. I still thought it was beautiful. My wife thought it was the stuff of nightmares.

Occasionally, in season (yes, there is a tarantula season), I see others of its species crossing the dirt road that leads to our property, and I wonder if my tarantula has returned. Do spiders have homing instincts? What was it looking for that drove it to somehow make its way into our house? If I looked hard enough at the right time of year, would I find waiting for me at the door leading to my study a little black-and-red valentine spun out of silk and the husks of dead insects?

When my wife tells friends that I'm a little strange, there are times when even I am compelled to concede the point.

* * *

Of all the carnivores that inhabit our fertile world perhaps none elicits such universal admiration as the bird of prey. Its actions are graceful, its profile noble, its devotion to mate and family admirable. So appealing are these birds in appearance and action that we often tend to forget that they are killers as ruthless and determined as any laughing hyena or spitting cobra. Perhaps part of this willful emotional disconnect is that they kill silently. A kestrel standing atop a dead vole with its talons embedded deep in the dead rodent's body may emit a high-pitched squeal or two, but its terse declamation of triumph is a long way from the lion's repetitive roars or the grizzly's incessant snarl.

Of course, snakes also kill in silence, but like the spider and the army ant, they lack the innate visual appeal of their lethal feathered counterparts. Birds of prey make frequent appearances on the currency, heraldic shields, and national symbology of numerous nations. They are the supermodels of the predator world. How often do you see a snake heroically portrayed thus, let alone a spider or carnivorous beetle? A snake does make an appearance on the flag of Mexico—as it is being snatched up by an eagle.

We cannot help ourselves, I suppose. What appears strikingly attractive to the human eye might look otherwise to an alien, who would perhaps favor the silhouette of the lamprey to that of the falcon. Beauty is in the eye of the beholding species. I sometimes wonder what the birds of prey think of *our* appearance.

I've always dreamed of seeing a harpy eagle. Discounting vultures such as the condor, the harpy and the Philippine eagle are the world's two largest birds of prey. Much larger, though, was the *Harpagornis moorei,* or Haast's eagle. Living in New Zealand and preying on the large flightless moas, it is estimated the last *Harpagornis* died out as recently as A.D. 1400. With a body weight of roughly thirty pounds and a ten-foot wing-span, it was big enough to bring down and prey on young humans. By way of comparison, a full-grown female bald eagle's weight maxes out at fourteen pounds with a wingspan of maybe six and a half feet.

I know that I am not going to see a live Haast's eagle any more than I'm likely to see a moa—though the rediscovery and resurrection of the turkey-size, flightless New Zealand bird called the takahe offers a last, lingering hope that a remnant population of small moas might yet some-how survive in the cloud-shrouded wilderness of Aotearoa's South Island. Slim though it is, I have a much better chance of one day encountering a harpy or a Philippine eagle than one of the flightless New Zealand giants, which sadly are no moa.

Bald eagles, now, those are comparatively easy to see since the dra-matic recovery of their breeding population in the United States. They even live in and around my hometown of Prescott. Visiting remote parts of the world has allowed me to see their close cousins, the other fish eagles, on multiple occasions. The most striking encounter occurred in the Raja Ampat Islands of eastern Indonesia. We were in a small boat wending our way through the remarkable karst landscape when a large sea eagle descended to its nest atop a jutting pinnacle of heavily eroded limestone. The eagle itself was striking, but its chosen perch even more so. The rock had been eroded to leave behind, from our viewing angle, the perfect silhouette of an eagle's head.

Though they do not attract as much notice as their flashier relative the bald eagle, fish eagles and ospreys are just as attractive to watch in the wild. Skimming along above the shining surface of still water, salt or fresh, they strike sharply downward with their claws at fish that are swimming just below the surface. Their wing beats grow stronger and more determined as they fight to climb skyward with their prey while simultaneously keeping watch for gulls or other scavengers that tend to linger close by, eager to snatch away the catch of another.

Some fish eagles have it easier than others. Those patrolling the sur-faces of lagoons in the Pacific have little to worry about. While hunting above rivers in the Amazon, fish-seeking raptors must keep an eye out for the occasional lurking caiman. I've always thought those that live in Africa have the hardest time of all.

Journeying upstream in a small boat on the Chobe River, which divides Botswana from the thin latitudinal ribbon of Namibia called the Caprivi Strip, I once watched a fish eagle hunting nearly parallel to our craft. Unlike its cousins elsewhere, it periodically had to rise and then drop down again in its quest for a meal, lest it run headlong into wrestling elephants, waiting crocodiles, migrating Cape buffalo, or the occasional gaping mouth of a yawning hippo. The eagle negotiated every one of these obstacles with equanimity, only intermittently venting its irritation with a piercing cry of indignation.

When it finally succeeded in snatching a fish from the roiling waters, it immediately retired to the top of the nearest suitable tree to consume its meal at leisure. As we motored past, the great bird looked up long enough to favor my guide and me with a suitably imperious glance before returning to its meal of fresh flesh and fish guts.

Residing where I do, on a small piece of undisturbed land on the fringes of an explosively expanding community, I have still had the occasional opportunity to observe such regal raptors at closer quarters than do my more urbanized friends. My study overlooks a small canyon through which runs a live stream. While like everything else that moves in Arizona the creek's cheerful rush is sometimes stilled by the anvil-like heat of high summer, there is almost always water present in shaded pools and secluded nooks in the sheltering granite. This permanent water source draws many prey species as well as those that prey upon them. Among these visitors can be counted the preferred diet of hawks, falcons, kestrels, and owls. Alas, the peregrine falcons that breed on nearby Granite Mountain prefer different quarry.

Over the years, I have grown intimate with an extended family of red-tailed hawks (*Buteo jamaicensis*) that nest in one of the ponderosa pines upslope from our house. I have never climbed the hill to the base of their tree in spring to observe the newborn young—I don't want to do anything to disturb them. Perhaps in gratitude, the offspring and their parents show little shyness when hunting on the property we share.

It is difficult to imagine anything more capable of distracting someone from his work than the sight of a full-grown red-tailed hawk streaking past the window. As my chair sits but a few feet from the glass and the gimlet-eyed patrolling raptor rockets by barely a couple of yards away on the other side of it, the occurance is more than sufficient to break my concentration no matter how often it happens. Now and then, the hawk will glance through the glass in my direction. I treasure each such encounter far more than any work it may have cost me.

I have watched while the hawks dive on prey; sometimes successfully, more often not. Once, walking around to the rear of our house, I found one sitting on one of our patio benches busily disemboweling a rabbit. It stayed there, intent on its meal, until my motionless staring presence must have finally disturbed it enough so that it flew off, its ragged meal hanging limply from its talons. The reason for its departure was wholly mine. I take the blame entirely.

Nobody likes to be gawked at while they're eating.

The roof of my study once boasted a large, old-fashioned, but at the time necessary UHF television antenna. After years of faithful service, the picture it delivered began to deteriorate until it became unwatchable. A technician I spoke to suggested there might be a problem with the antenna. There was.

Having apparently decided that at least for a change the feel of aluminum against its feet was preferable to that of wood, one of our resident red-tailed hawks had been utilizing the antenna on a daily basis as a suitable place from which to keep watch on the nearby creek. I tolerated the situation until it grew bored of the spot. Then I changed the antenna, opting in the process for one significantly less perchlike in design. My television reception improved immediately, and I am sure the raptor did not go hungry.

* * *

I frequently work on into the night. One cool autumn's eve I emerged from my study to see something sizable occupying the middle of our driveway. In the fading light I at first took it to be a package that had fallen out of our car. I am sure the owl that I mistook for a misplaced grocery bag would have been grievously insulted at the gaffe.

It was a great horned owl *(Bubo virginianus)*, huge of eye and robust of body. What was it doing standing on the ground in our driveway? As I approached, advancing as patiently as I could, it continued to pose there gazing back at me. The body and the great wings were the color of steel flecked with obsidian. The bird was huge, stunning. As I came closer, advancing hunched over and taking short steps, it opened its beak and yelled at me: *Kree-elp, kree-elp!* Was it hurt? Its wings and body appeared undamaged. Perhaps it was sick, or just old. Possibly . . .

"It'll take your finger off."

Emerging from the house, JoAnn had come up the driveway to look for me and had instead come upon this entirely unexpected bird-husband encounter.

I halted my advance. The owl's beak and talons appeared to be in as good condition as the rest of him. While I wanted to pick up the bird, to check it for buckshot or wire, to calm it, I knew that JoAnn was right. The owl was not likely to respond to my touch by lying back and closing its eyes. It was much more apt to react defensively.

"We could call the vet," I suggested.

She sighed. "It's after hours. Maybe the forest service." She indicated the silently staring visitor. "If it's still here tomorrow."

I nodded. "I know, I know." As usual, where animals were concerned, JoAnn had voiced the right thing to do.

She turned to go back to the house. "It's getting dark. And cold. Are you coming?"

"In a little while."

I stayed with the great horned owl for at least another hour. Crouched on the ground, gazing into vast yellow eyes that often blinked and turned away from me, I struggled to make that absurd and illogical connection that humans often attempt when confronted with a representative of the waning wild. We are so sure that if we just try hard enough we can understand, we can communicate with wild animals. Everyone likes to think they are special, especially when it comes to establishing a relationship with other species. The thing of it is, other species usually don't want to establish a relationship with us. If they did, they would no longer be wild. We have domesticated enough of the natural world, to serve us both as companions and as food.

Straightening, I bid our enigmatic guest good night, rose, and made a wide circle around it as I walked down to the house.

An hour later and still consumed with curiosity, I returned to check on our visitor. It was gone. Searching the area with my flashlight, I could find no sign of him. No dropped or plucked feathers, no blood, nothing to indicate it was in any way injured or had been harmed. A mystery, but one with, to all intents and purposes, a happy ending. Returning to the house, I felt a lot better about the situation.

Maybe, I told myself, *the owl had swallowed a mouse that hadn't agreed with it. Or eaten some spoiled food a thoughtless homeowner had left out for neighborhood cats.* Or maybe it had just been in the mood to sit on the ground for a while and stare at whomever happened to amble along. Hoo knows?

Two final owlish observations: the great horned owls, like the hawks, are permanent residents in our canyon. Many a summer's night, we see them sitting in their favorite trees and hear them hooting back and forth. I have tried hooting at them in turn, and flatter myself that they answer me. In reality, they are doubtless just continuing to call among themselves, no doubt saying something like, "Don't you wish that stupid mammal would just *shut up*?"

And the other thing I have learned about great horned owls . . . ?

You cannot imagine the sheer volume of their nightly defecations, the kitchen-sink whiteness of it, and how hard it can be to try and remove the stuff from patio flagstone once it has had a chance to dry. It sets like tub grout. The daily output of an entire flock of pigeons does not begin to compare.

IX

EYES ON THE TRAIL

Central Gabon, January 2007

CARNIVORE OR HERBIVORE?

When you walk through the rain forest and suddenly encounter nothing but an eye or two staring back at you, when you can see nothing but unmoving pupil and glassy reflection and no body, how do you tell whether the animal behind the eye desires to eat you, avoid you, or a little of both? It frequently depends on circumstance, conditions, your presumed palatability on the part of the eye's owner, and a dozen or more other variables. All of them usually beyond your control.

The forests of central Gabon are among the least disturbed remaining in Africa. This is because Gabon is fortunate in having a low population-to-land ratio compared to many of its neighbors, boasts a fair amount of mountainous terrain unsuitable for easy slash-and-burn agriculture, and has managed to utilize at least some of the money acquired from the sale of its oil for purposes other than lining the pockets of its leaders, or "big men" as they are often called in Africa. The country also generates substantial income from the sale of forest products, yet remains percentage-wise one of the most forested countries on Earth.

All of this allows for the existence of national parks that in many places actually serve the function of national parks instead of private preserves for local exploiters. Within their boundaries, I have been fortunate to see some of Gabon's many animal wonders: elephants foraging on beaches fronting the surf-tossed Atlantic; large primates like the black-capped mangabey and black colobus monkey that do not automatically flee at the sight of a human; the forest buffalo (smaller than their Cape cousins); and the outrageous red river hog, which with the white stripe down its back, facial bumps, long tufted ears, striking rust-red coloring, and the porcine equivalent of a Fu Manchu mustache, looks like a giant pig that's been tricked out by a southern California custom car shop. I have seen hippo tracks on the beach (though alas, not their makers in the water) and chimpanzees in the forests of Loango. In Lopé National Park, a startled young silverback gorilla once paced our 4x4 for half a mile, astonishing us not only with its endurance but its speed.

But of all Gabon's mammalian wonders, none is more intriguing than the forest elephant. No, it's not a predator, but its size, elusiveness, and temperament make it more of a real threat to visitors than the scarce leopard or gentle gorilla.

My sister and I were staying at the Tassi Camp, a tented facility located a full day's drive over rain-soaked tracks from the main lodge at Loango. Tassi is situated on the crest of a gentle slope overlooking damp, muddy, flat ground interspersed with sizable patches of dense forest. A short drive westward leads to uninhabited coast that is in full view of the camp. I went bodysurfing there one day, the only recreational swimmer for dozens of miles in either direction, too content to worry about sharks and the far more potentially dangerous medical debris that arrives on the current from the mouth of the Congo River not far to the south.

Our guide had been brought in from his own well-established safari operation in Zambia to help expand and professionalize the still very new tourist facilities in Loango. Though hailing originally from New Zealand, he had long since joined the community of the African bush, a neighborhood that knows no nationality save Nature. Quickly discerning that I was not a fresh-faced insurance salesman from Des Moines embarking on his first visit to the jungle, he artfully shifted his ongoing narration away from tourist generalities and became more specific and conversational. It was not necessary for him, for example, to instruct my sister and me to avoid picking up snakes or going for a hike sans full water bottle and something to eat.

Tassi is a strange place to trek. Every step you take on the open, rain-saturated terrain, you are likely to see your feet sink into muck and mud that sometimes swallows you halfway to your knees. In every direction, clumps of forest beckon. The sodden air within their boundaries is no less humid than that out on the flat coastal plain, but at least the leaves and branches of the trees offer some protection from direct sunlight. It was within these mottled woods that one morning we caught a glimpse of stocky black shapes traveling in a line. Wild chimps. A big male glanced once in our direction, and then they were gone.

My experience in similar surroundings notwithstanding, our guide (like any guide) had his ground rules. The one he repeated more often than any other was, "Forest elephants can be almost invisible. If we should happen to surprise any, whatever you do, *don't run*." Along with a handful of other rules, this admonition was repeated every time we set out for a walk.

I soon surmised that the urgency with which this caution was repeated might have something to do with a local forest elephant the staff at the camp had nicknamed Cruella. While the other amiable members of her foraging family group were content to avoid the open camp, Cruella had concluded that there was food to be had within. Whenever visitors arrived, she would magically appear that same night to try and force her way into the food lockers. With no substantial structure at hand in which to secure supplies, the staff had taken to placing the lockers high up in a tree sturdy enough to be elephant-proof. This primitive but highly effective ploy did not sit well with Cruella.

Our first midnight at Tassi, we were awakened by the sounds of shouting and the repeated loud honking and engine-revving of our four-wheel drive. Fumbling for a flashlight, I stumbled out of my cot and to the entrance of our tent. It turned out that I didn't need the light. Less than a hundred yards away, a frustrated Cruella was confronting our Land Cruiser. With half the camp staff on board, it charged at her repeatedly. The driver revved the engine as loudly as he could while everyone in the open back end stood wildly waving their arms and yelling at the tops of their lungs. The aggravated elephant would make a charge, halt abruptly, flare her ears, trumpet her resentment, and then retreat, whereupon the entire process would repeat itself, only with her now positioned farther from the camp.

Standing in the tent opening, my sister and I watched this peculiarly African ballet for about an hour until Cruella, furious and defeated, turned and stomped off into the nearest patch of forest.

On previous travels, I had been variously awakened from a sound sleep by the plaintive wail of emergency sirens, the carousing of drunken revelers, bawling lions, high seas, and, in Saint Petersburg, an attractive Russian hooker mistakenly sent to my room by a member of the staff at the hotel where I happened to be staying who hoped I might be in need of some nocturnal company. But never before by an elephant dueling with a car.

Cruella had her revenge, though. Slipping quietly into camp the following night, she proceeded to pummel her tormentor mercilessly, bending the driver's side rearview mirror in half and putting one of her tusks right through the windshield on the passenger side. Viewing such damage, one suspects there must be places in Africa where you can buy elephant insurance for your vehicle.

While this destruction formed the basis for some predictable light banter on the day following Cruella's Revenge, as it quickly came to be called, it was not taken lightly as we set out on our last morning's hike at Tassi. Out on the open, bumpy, muddy surface, we could see for miles, but we knew we would have to be more cautious when we entered the patchwork forest. Somewhere in our immediate neighborhood brooded one seriously dyspeptic pachyderm, whom none of us had any desire to surprise.

When possible, all safari walks in Africa are done in the morning and the late afternoon, not only to avoid the heat of midday but because the animals do the same and those are the best times for wildlife sightings. As we walked, we encountered some red river hogs, a pair of sitatungas, and the usual exotic birds, but for the most part, that morning at Tassi tended toward tranquillity. As the sun rose, the humidity increased along with it. Off to my right, I could hear but not see the booming surf. With each boggy step, the thought of another dip in the ocean increased its appeal.

We were hiking out on the mucky, treeless flats parallel to a clump of forest. As with all tropical forests, wherever there is an absence of trees, the undergrowth explodes to produce what appears to be a solid wall of green. This is no reflection on the equal fecundity of the forest's interior, which often boasts ample room between individual boles in which to walk, but rather has to do with the much greater availability of unobstructed sunlight. This is why tropical rivers appear to be lined with impenetrable jungle. Every square inch of space is filled with verdure as plants on the fringes of forest or growing along riverbanks take every advantage of the precious, unblocked, energy-producing sunshine. As we walked, our guide was searching the green barrier on our right for a suitable place where we could enter.

In the motionless water-heavy air, the thunderous blast of sound that erupted from the trees resounded as loudly as Gabriel's horn announcing the apocalypse—except that this herald came equipped with her own built-in trumpet. I thought instantly of the bent side-view mirror and the hole in the tough glass of the Land Cruiser's windshield. Our guide's reaction was instantaneous.

"RUN!" he yelled at the top of his lungs as he turned to his left and burst into a mad sprint perpendicular to the trees.

I started to comply, only to have my leg pause literally halfway off the ground as I gaped at him in confusion. My sister stood frozen, her gaze darting rapidly back and forth between guide and brother. I don't think I stammered.

"But you said not to run under any circumstan—"

"Run, run!" He slowed his pace long enough to look back at the trees and at us, but he did not stop.

Unsurprisingly, we ran.

A couple of hundred yards away, we were forced to stop to catch our breath. Perspiration poured down the length of our bodies like slender threads of channeled whitewater. Looking back at the section of forest we had been a mere couple of steps from entering, we saw nothing. No movement, and no sign of whichever elephant had startled us into anxious flight.

"Cruella?" Bent over with her hands on her knees, my sister was panting hard, but she hadn't fallen. As was her preference, she had been hiking barefoot.

"Possibly." Our guide was studying the motionless trees intently, still not wholly content with the distance we had put between them and ourselves. "No way of telling unless she comes out."

"How close were we?" my sister asked.

I looked at her, then I looked at our guide. He looked at me.

"Too close," he said. "A matter of feet, not yards. She was right there, just inside the first branches."

I had not seen so much as a trace of elephant. I did my best not to sound accusing. "You told us not to run."

He didn't hesitate. "Almost every time, you *don't* run. Ninety-eight percent of the time, you don't run." He nodded in the direction of the trees from whence the overwhelming blast of sound had originated. "But when you're that close, you run. Might well have been a mother with a calf. Just letting us know we were getting too close."

As we slugged down the contents of our water bottles, a part of me was sorry we had not seen the elephant in question. It would have been interesting to know its identity. And while I realize that I am succumbing to easy anthropomorphizing, I cannot escape this image of Cruella, lying on her back in the forest with her forelegs crossed over her chest, trunk in the air, laughing some self-satisfied, uncontrollable, elephant laugh.

* * *

Mikongo Camp lies not in the Congo but deep within Lopé National Park in the center of Gabon. Its simple but sturdy individual wooden chalets boast showers, large beds, and plenty of mosquito netting, though nothing can keep rain-forest bugs completely out of any building. As you go about your business, you learn to dance around the potentially dangerous ones, admire the attractive ones, and ignore the ants. It's their forest, after all.

With a pair of dedicated trackers, we were off searching for mountain lowland gorillas. As the hours wore on and we found ourselves struggling up and down mud-slicked jungle paths, we found plenty of gorilla spoor but were unable to catch up to the local group itself. We were advancing along a trail cut into the side of a steep hill when my sister stopped in front of me. Intent on keeping watch for insects and other denizens of the forest floor (we had encountered a young green mamba the day before), it dawned on me that not only had everyone stopped, but they had gone completely silent.

Then I saw our lead guide gesturing for us to back up.

I had been on numerous jungle walks with a wide assortment of guides on four continents and had been their recipient of a full compliment of hand gestures, but this was the first time one of them had ever indicated I needed to back up. The other guide had placed a finger against his lips in the universal signal for silence.

From my position at the back of the line, I strained to see past them. Around us, the trees rang with the symphony of the forest: unseen chattering monkeys, the occasional cry of a bird that was a flash of iridescence as it darted between branches, the electronic whine of cicadas. Buttressed boles fought their neighbors for precious sunlight. Spreading its wings and thereby surrendering its camouflage, an audacious butterfly shone sapphire as it briefly exposed itself like a Manhattan flasher. All about us there was sound, no fury, and little movement.

Peering past the heads of my sister and our guides, I could see nothing in front of them but leaves, twigs, and trees. What had brought about such an abrupt halt to our hike? Straining to make out any disruption to the all-pervasive greenery, I finally saw it. A single eye, gazing back in our general direction. That was all, just an eye. An eye topped by lashes as elegant as any curled in a Beverly Hills beauty salon, only considerably

141

longer than those favored by the most outrageous drag queen. No other eye has lashes like that, or is as likely to be found so high off the ground.

Behind the eye was a forest elephant.

Though less than ten yards distant, I could not see anything else of its owner. The elephant blended in completely with the surrounding forest. Unlike their more recognizable East and South African relatives, the forest elephant of central Africa (*Loxodonta cyclotis*) is smaller, has rounder ears, tusks that tend to point downward and are composed of harder ivory than that of other elephants, and five toes on its front feet and four on the back as opposed to its savanna-dwelling relatives, which have one less toe on each foot.

I badly wanted to put a number of questions to our guides, but I kept silent. Stuck on the flank of a steep, slippery, jungle-encrusted hill, we had nowhere to run if the elephant decided to charge. So we stood utterly motionless for long moments, not all the sweat that was pouring off us a consequence of the heat and humidity.

Five minutes passed without anyone saying a word. The time had doubled when our lead guide gestured that we could advance, albeit slowly and carefully. A few minutes later, we stopped by an opening in the brush that intersected our trail. Kneeling, the guide pointed out broken branches and spoor.

"Elephant make this trail. The forest is full of them." He grinned as he rose. "But they like to use our trails, too."

Once more, I had occasion to reflect on the silence of elephants. Be they inhabitants of the open plains of East or South Africa, the deserts of Namibia, or the forests of the Congo Basin, they wear a hush like an overcoat and move with a silence that never fails to astonish. In the deep jungle, you can pass within feet of one and never know it's there. The smaller species are the graceful gray ghosts of the forest, and it is a pity they are less well known than their larger African and Southeast Asian cousins.

And it is a very good thing for those who choose to go for a stroll among their haunts that they are strict vegetarians. . . .

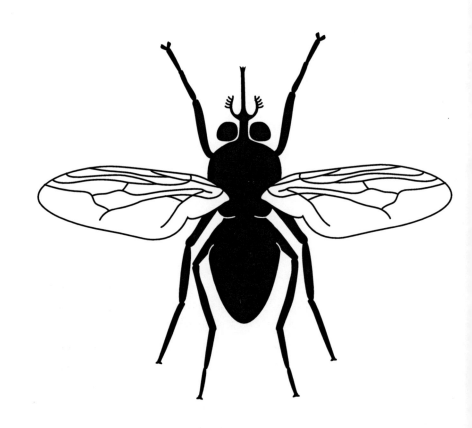

X

EVER WONDER HOW *WE* TASTE?

Papua New Guinea, October 1995

NORTH OF PORT MORESBY, THE capital of Papua New Guinea, lies the most accessible of that remarkable country's national parks—accessibility in such a region being a relative term. PNG's second largest metropolitan area, Lae, is technically just as accessible as the capital, if one overlooks the fact that for a sizable, developed city it may boast the largest concentration of car-swallowing potholes in the world. I am not exaggerating. The combination of unstable ground, tropical soils, a seaside setting, insufficient financing for infrastructure repair, and fierce rain creates cavities in the frail urban pavement that in other countries would be referred to not as potholes but as cave-ins.

From Mosby, as its inhabitants like to call it, to Varirata National Park it's a good half-day's drive in a sturdy 4x4. Ascending from sea level to more than 2,500 feet, the Sogeri Road soon becomes a dirt track and, if it hasn't rained too hard or too recently, stays passable as it follows the course of the rushing Laloki River. Along the way, you are likely to encounter farmers and traders and just possibly, *raskols*, PNG's infamous bandits and all-around antisocial types. As compensation, Varirata offers a distinctly cooler climate than Mosby in addition to the opportunity to see some of PNG's fabulous wildlife while still keeping a base in the capital city. From several designated vantage points, there are also spectacular views out over the city and across Bootless Bay.

I had come up to Varirata in hopes of seeing a few of the birds for which PNG is justly renowned. Among them can be counted the Goura pigeon—the world's largest—and a vast variety of songbirds. The park being located so close to the city, I did not hold out hopes for seeing anything especially unusual. I did not expect to have an encounter with something as rare, for example, as a black leopard.

Journey in expectation of seeing nothing, and you will invariably be surprised.

Since there were no regular tours to Varirata, I had hired a car and driver. Edward was not a guide, though he was willing to accompany me into the forest—for an additional fee, of course. The trails in Varirata being well marked and reasonably well maintained, I decided instead to head off for a couple of hours on my own. Many of my most memorable rain-forest encounters have taken place when I was by myself. The less noise you make, the less disturbance you create, the less presence you bring, the better your chances of seeing something out of the ordinary. Conversation with fellow humans I can get anytime.

Trekking Varirata involved some up-and-down hiking, but I came across no slopes that proved particularly strenuous. While it was indeed cooler than down on the coast in Port Morseby, I was still in the tropics and soon found myself drenched in familiar perspiration. I was wearing what at that time I thought was appropriate attire: short-sleeved shirt, shorts, and sandals. Having liberally dosed myself with insect repellant, I considered myself reasonably well defended from mosquitoes. Varirata was not the Amazon. While present, the park's mossies (as the Australians call them) were nothing like the anemia-inducing hordes I had encountered elsewhere.

Though the forest was relatively open, I stayed on the trail. Since within a mature rain forest, everything looks exactly the same in every direction, you can walk twenty feet off a trail and quickly find yourself hopelessly lost. Small streambeds present another danger, since when dry they often resemble trails and can easily lead the unwary astray. I was entirely alone. Varirata is not Yellowstone (though it was that American park that directly inspired Varirata's creation). Spectacular, enormous birdwing butterflies soared overhead, as if someone was periodically shaking Christmas tree ornaments out of the rain-forest canopy. As I walked, I kept a wary eye out for snakes. In some countries, poisonous serpents have been bequeathed innocuous names, like the deadly but blandly named Australian brown snake. In New Guinea, you have the death adder. There's a reptile whose name would not lead to unnecessary queries as to its lethal potential.

You want to walk quietly in the rain forest, but with a heavy step. Exceptionally sensitive to vibration, a snake detecting your approach is eager to slither off into the brush and out of your path. It's the terrestrial equivalent of shuffling your feet in shallow water to alert any dozing stingrays.

Weird cries from unseen sources intrigued but did not unsettle me. One was especially loud and sharp. It struck me that this was because the sound was now coming from almost directly overhead. Tilting back my head, I searched the trees, squinting at the occasional burst of sunlight that thrust down between the branches. Something was moving among the leaves. It was sizable, mostly golden-brown in color, with a tail that more than anything else resembled a Persian potentate's fly whisk.

Raggiana bird of paradise.

I had never seen a bird of paradise in the wild, though I had hoped to do so. Here, not far over my head, was the national bird of Papua New Guinea, indifferent to my gawking presence and busily squawking its head off. I struggled with my camera. The Raggiana is not an especially rare bird of paradise, but for someone whose most common avian acquaintances are canyon towhees and blue jays, it was as alien as a pterodactyl.

What I did not realize, in my excitement and enchantment, was that I was standing still as I was recording video. And while I was standing still, certain denizens of the rain forest were not.

I was not alerted to the presence of my fellow traveler until I was back in my hotel room and stripping off my sweat-sodden clothes preparatory to climbing into the shower. I took off my right sandal and was working on the heel strap of its companion when I noticed something dark brown, almost black, clinging to the top of my left foot. It glistened. Thinking it a curled leaf, I brushed at it and was startled to find that a) it didn't move, and b) it was cylindrical and solid, albeit a bit on the pulpy side. I bent over for a closer look. Though this was my initial encounter with one of the little literal hangers-on, I knew now what it was.

My first leech.

If I had not looked directly at it, I would never have known it was there. I felt nothing: no weight, and certainly no discomfort. About an inch and a half long and the thickness of a small pencil, it clung contentedly to my foot, sucking away in silence. I'm sure had I ignored it, it would have concluded its meal quite contentedly and dropped off without my ever having become aware of its presence.

I am ashamed to say I reacted like the extra in a bad movie who always dies first. You know the type: the non-lead character who is constantly scanning the jungle nervously muttering dialogue like, "This is a bad place, sir, a bad place. The natives here say that this forest is haunted by evil spirits, and that no one who goes in is ever seen again." The leads turn away momentarily, we hear a high-pitched scream, and . . .

Guess which character gets chomped by a jaguar, or strangled by an anaconda, or eaten in his sleep by army ants.

I flailed wildly at the leech. Unlike as with so many other creatures in this book, I did so without pausing to study its behavior or striving to recall its scientific nomenclature. For those of you who live in places like New York or Chicago or London and have to deal with leeches every day and therefore are in desperate need of this vital information, there are several ways to get a leech to drop harmlessly off your body. Apply insect repellent (DEET works), salt, vinegar, lemon juice, vinegar, or tobacco spit. If none of these is available, place a lighted match next to the leech. The best method involves no chemical intervention at all. Press your finger against your skin and slide the nail up against the back end of the sucker, breaking its suction hold on your body. When that happens, it will usually release its bite, whereupon you can then pick it up and flick it away.

I am abashed to admit that in the heat of the moment I had put every one of these recommended remedies completely out of my mind. All I could think of was an unshaven, exhausted Humphrey Bogart slogging through the reeds dragging Katherine Hepburn and the *African Queen* behind him: indisputably the most memorable sequence involving leeches in the entire history of film.

My frantic shoves finally succeeded in knocking the little sucker off. As it writhed and twisted on the floor, seeking a purchase—seeking me—it left behind a small bloody circle on my foot. Disdaining my usual scientific approach, I flushed the parasitic invader without a moment's concern for the life of another living creature.

Thanks to the anticoagulants secreted by the leech, the circle bled longer than was usual for such a small infringement. But before too long, the bleeding stopped and the spot healed over. I have a scar there to this day: a reminder that where parasites are concerned, it is always best to act with patience and knowledge and not in haste. It also serves as a reminder of something important for anyone who wants to ensure their safety while battling their way through damp jungle. A critical precaution that should be adhered to no matter how oppressive the heat and the humidity.

Forget the elephant gun. Leave behind the Bowie knife. The machete is useful but not essential.

Wear socks.

* * *

Tanzania, July 1984

WHAT HALTED THE ADVANCE AND the spread of nomadic cattle herders across all of East and Southern Africa was not intertribal warfare, nor the arrival of Arab slavers or European colonists, nor a shortage of adequate pasturage or water for their animals. It was, as is so often the case throughout human history, a disease. And in this instance, a disease that affects cattle and cattle herders alike.

African trypanosomiasis is far less benign than the name it is commonly known by: sleeping sickness.

Besides obliterating cattle by the herd, this exceedingly unpleasant affliction was for many years the number-one cause of death among the human population in some parts of Africa. Once infected, a person begins to suffer fever, headache, and joint pain. Swelling of the lymph nodes, sometimes to prodigious size, follows. Left untreated, the disease spreads throughout the body and methodically overwhelms its defenses. It starts to affect the brain, manifesting itself in bouts of confusion and a complete disruption of the normal sleep cycle, which leads eventually to coma and death. Survivors often suffer permanent neurological damage, including at least one variety of Parkinson's disease. The disease is caused by the introduction of the protozoan *Trypanosoma,* into the bloodstream of cattle and humans. The protozoan itself is transmitted to cattle and their herders by the tsetse fly.

If sleeping sickness is a benign malady, give me malaria.

Having read about Africa all my life, I had naturally come across innumerable references to the tsetse fly and to sleeping sickness. So it was with some trepidation that when preparing to visit East Africa for the first time, I wrote our friend and host Bill Smythe to ask about whether or not the disease was present in any of the areas where we intended to travel.

"Plenty of tsetse flies," Bill replied, "but very little trypanosomiasis."

Good enough—I was half reassured. We booked our plane tickets.

Having driven through east and southern Tanzania for weeks without encountering the fabled vectors, we had grown somewhat complacent regarding the threat they posed. It was not until we headed north and found ourselves in the forest around Lake Manyara that they began to make their presence known—and to remind us why entire sections of Africa remain to this day unable to support herdsmen and their cattle.

We had stopped the car to watch a huge troop of baboons playing, feeding, and generally acting like primates. To conserve hard-to-obtain fuel, we had the air-conditioner off and the windows rolled down. Had any of the baboons approached too closely, we would have swiftly rolled them back up. Baboons are notorious for invading cars and making off with anything they can lay their hands on. But since we were off the beaten tourist track, this particular large troop was unsure of us. They had not yet learned that humans in cars can be a source of food and entertainment.

Suddenly, Sally Smythe let out a yelp of pain, and we all immediately looked in her direction.

"Tsetse fly," she declared unhappily. A moment later, JoAnn echoed our friend's exclamation. We immediately started rolling up windows— and embarking on a frenzied program of highly localized extermination.

We couldn't roll the windows down to shoo the flies out because that would only let more of them in. That was when I discovered that the tsetse fly is very likely the most intelligent and deceptive member of the fly family. It is certainly the toughest.

They're not hard to see. About the size of a common large housefly, they are the same bland gray in color; the better to blend in with any background, no doubt. They are also the possums of the fly world. Swat a tsetse fly, and it will fall off you, lie on the ground (or in this case the floor of the car) and play dead. Look away, and this Lazarusian insect immediately returns to the attack.

And it is just that, an attack. Even the vicious horsefly of the western United States takes a moment or two to evaluate its meal before dining, going for a stroll on its unsuspecting quarry while searching for a suitable place to dig in. The tsetse is far less discriminating. It doesn't land on you so much as it dives, needlelike proboscis fully extended, more swordsman than surgeon. Instead of touching down with its feet, it makes contact lance-first. Unlike the more well-mannered leech, which secretes painkiller along with anticoagulant, you are aware of the tsetse's presence on your body immediately. If the tsetse was an airplane, it would be a Luftwaffe Stuka.

A fiery pain lanced through my left arm. Startled, I swung on the fly with the flat of my right hand. Used to dealing with flies back home, I failed to put sufficient force behind the blow.

I kid you not. The fly staggered, but remained affixed to my flesh.

It was plain that clearing out the car wasn't going to be a simple matter of waving at flies. We were engaged in all-out combat.

I struck again, hard enough this time to bring redness to my skin. The tsetse dropped off, fell to the floor of the car, and lay there motionless. As yet unacquaintanted with the tsetse ruse, I immediately forgot about it. Big mistake.

I can't swear that the fly that stabbed into my ankle moments later was the same one I had knocked off my arm, but by that time I was no longer interested in the details of individual identification. All of us were swatting, yelping, trying to juggle car windows, and generally acting like unwilling participants in a cheap horror movie.

"You can't swat 'em," Bill advised us from his position behind the wheel. "You have to kill 'em. One at a time. And make sure they're dead."

JoAnn and I had already divined this bit of practical African lore for ourselves. The problem was, kill them with what? The heaviest, loudest hand-smack was capable of dislodging them, but after playing deader than a parrot in a Monty Python sketch, they swiftly returned to the attack. A book would have been ideal, preferably something weighty by Stephen King or Tom Clancy, but our books were locked in the trunk—and with a horde of tsetses swarming around the Subaru anxious to get inside, no one offered to step out to unpack suitable volumes. Several minutes of desperate slapping and hopeful experimentation passed before the ideal solution presented itself.

I had brought along a couple of Frisbees, to play with and to trade or give away (somewhere in southern Kenya there is a Masai chief who is the proud owner of an official authorized Batman Frisbee). We soon developed a first-rate method for exterminating tsetse flies that have invaded a vehicle. I reproduce it here for all who may have need of it in the near future.

1. Use Frisbee to trap tsetse fly against solid material such as a window or dashboard.

2. Apply pressure to Frisbee.

3. Push down until you hear something crunch.

Although we suffered some nasty bites, I am happy to report that none of us contracted trypanosomiasis. However, effective as this treatment for dealing with tsetses is, I have to confess that it does come with a pair of unfortunate side effects: dirty windows (there is a lot of blood in a tsetse fly) and one very messy Frisbee. A fair trade-off, though, for avoiding the pain and blood loss that results from a bite. Having personally and successfully applied this technique on multiple occasions at Lake Manyara, Tarangire, and points north in Tanzania, I therefore recommend the inclusion of an emergency Frisbee in the baggage of anyone contemplating travel to these regions. It's part of what you need to stay safe in the jungle and the savanna.

Socks and a Frisbee. Any caliber.

* * *

Southeastern Peru, May 1987: A Sartorial Digression

TO PROTECT YOURSELF FROM PREDATORY bloodsuckers, you obviously need more than good socks. Chapter and verse has been written and ample debate exists about what are the best clothes to wear in the depths of the rain forest. As is true of much in life, that which we learn most effectively and which sticks with us the longest we often find out by doing the wrong and not the right thing.

I certainly fulfilled that truism in the course of my first visit to real rain forest, in southeastern Peru.

Wear long pants, the written advisories said. Wear shirts with long sleeves.

What? In the steamy rain forest, where I knew I would be far more comfortable in shorts and a cut-off T-shirt? Though I pondered the alternatives, I reluctantly decided to go with the professional advice. But what kind of long pants and long-sleeved shirt? The closest climate I had experienced to that of the Amazon was French Polynesia, where the land-based predators are considerably reduced in number, species, and temperament. While sucking blood infused with a good pinot noir, even the mosquitoes I had encountered in the canyons of Moorea had evinced a decidedly laissez-faire attitude toward my mildly alcoholic presence.

But this was the Amazon I was heading for, not Tahiti. I resolved to prepare as best I could, given the information available to me. The troubles I soon experienced stemmed not from ignoring good advice but from not having read widely enough.

In 1987, not a great deal was known about Manú. There was no place to stay in or near the park and no Internet that would allow one to readily draw upon the limited amount of information that was available. With no experience in true jungle travel and no one else in my family or circle of friends who had ever been closer to such a place than the Enchanted Tiki Room at Disneyland, I was on my own.

I decided not to invest money that I did not have anyway in specialized attire I might never use again. Surely, a good pair of jeans would suffice to keep off the insects, and if the mosquitoes were really bad I could swap out a T-shirt for one of several well-used long-sleeved dress shirts. So when my friend Mark and I made our arrangements in Cusco to go down into Manú, clothing-wise I felt reasonably well prepared.

It took less than a day for me to realize that I had no idea what I was in for.

There are several reasons why much of the Manú region of southeastern Peru has remained to this day in a virtually untouched state of natural bliss. Difficulty of access is one. Expense in getting there is another. But access and expense won't keep out rogue loggers, illegal gold miners, and experienced animal poachers. What will keep them out are some of the most fearsome arthropods in the entire Amazon basin.

I've written about the vicious, headfirst attack of the tsetse fly and the subtle depredation of the leech. In Manú, I encountered something I have yet to come across anywhere else: bloodsucking insects that can bite through denim. At first, I was reluctant to believe it was happening. But the welts I rapidly acquired on my thighs and other "protected" areas quickly persuaded me. These had not been inflicted by chiggers, mites, ticks, or other parasitic creatures that had crawled under my jeans and up my legs. Never having heard of permethrin, I had not appropriately sprayed any of my clothing with that useful chemical prior to my departure for the hinterlands. My long-sleeved dress shirts proved equally powerless to blunt the daily attacks. Furthermore, they were heavy and hot to the point of suffocation.

I now understood why all the locals wore shorts and T-shirts. It was not because they were immune to the bites and stings, though they were certainly more habituated to them than I was. It was just that anything they could buy or afford locally would have provided little in the way of a defense against the biting insects they were forced to confront every hour of their lives. And if you're going to get chewed up and spit out anyway, you might as well be as cool about it as possible while you're being slowly devoured by dozens of tiny, determined, biting creatures.

I had brought along what I thought would serve as excellent protection; repellent that was 100 percent DEET. While this chemical has continued to prove its effectiveness against a multitude of bugs throughout the world, it failed me miserably in Manú. Contrastingly, there is no telling what would have happened to me without it. The problem with DEET in its purer concentrations is that it is exceptionally powerful stuff. I learned this when my sticky, repellent-slathered hands left permanent fingerprints on the metal housing of my 35-mm camera. Tests run years later by the U.S. Army disclosed that a repellent containing 29 to 33 percent DEET is the ideal formulation. Anything less results in reduced effectiveness, and greater concentrations provide little or no additional protection against biting insects.

When I returned home, my wife took one peep at me and nearly picked up the phone to call the doctor. I looked, I am not ashamed to say, like someone who had contracted every disease the Amazon had to offer, in addition to some colorful decorative flourishes added by a deranged but especially imaginative artist. Think someone struck by the measles and chickenpox at the same time. I itched like a madman for several weeks until the splotches, blotches, and other visible marks of my South American sojourn finally faded away. We all like to lose a little weight now and then, but there are more efficient and less debilitating methods of doing it.

The next time I was preparing to visit rain forest (in this case, Papua New Guinea), I thoroughly researched appropriate clothing. A company named Willis & Geiger that had been making safari gear for almost a hundred years boasted of clothing woven from a custom lightweight cotton twill that breathed well and was tough enough to turn back the jaws of an army ant. I bought a pair of their shorts, a pair of long pants, and a long-sleeved shirt. I have them still. With the exception of having to replace two buttons, they are as sound as the day I first wore them. No thorn has ever pierced the material nor any bug, no matter how determined, penetrated the fabric to reach my skin. Additionally, in this specialized attire, I can walk all day in the rain forest, soak it through with perspiration, hang it up in a hotel room, and wear the same outfit to dinner that night in a nice restaurant without embarrassing myself.

So naturally, the company is now out of business, having been purchased by a much bigger concern that promptly discontinued the special material because, as was explained to me by a company executive, "The market for this sort of specialized apparel is too small." I wouldn't trade my set of well-worn Willis & Geiger for the finest suit on Saville Row.

After all, when it comes to repelling bugs with jaws the size of your fingernails and the temperament of a testosterone-crazed ultimate fighter, you're far better off setting aside the silk and satin.

XI

EATING, YAWNING, AND COITUS INTERRUPTUS

Northern Botswana, October 1993

THERE ARE TIMES WHEN THE encounters experienced in a single day can overwhelm a traveler with a multitude of memorable incidents the full effects of which are realized only on later reflection. It's a matter of timing, planning, and luck. Everything that follows occurred in the same small corner of Botswana, involved the same predator species, and happened over the course of a single fifteen-hour period. Though they followed swiftly one upon another in a blur of blood and teeth and confusion, all are now forever individually etched in my mind. It shows that if you take the time and make the effort to get a little way off the beaten path and away from other travelers, any number of special moments can be had in a short period of time.

I have previously mentioned Chobe National Park. Chobe has perhaps the greatest concentration of elephants in all of Africa. The population varies according to season, the skill of those doing the counting, the weather, and numerous other factors, but at any one time or another the country may be home to as few as 20,000 or as many as 50,000 elephants. Since much of Botswana is desert, a majority of them can often be found hanging out on the banks of the perennial Chobe River.

Viewing elephants at the Chobe can be done from the top of a Unimog, a massive four-wheel drive vehicle capable of ferrying as many as twenty or more chattering tourists at a time over and through nearly any terrain its expansive wheelbase can span. The herds (of elephants, not tourists) can be better viewed from an open jeep in the company of just seven or eight fellow travelers. But if you have a little money that you're willing to spend on something besides a bigger TV, fancier tequila, or that custom speaker setup for your car, some unpreprogammed travel time, and a deep and abiding interest in what you supposedly have actually come all the way to Africa to see, most places you can make arrangements to hire your own jeep and driver. That's what I did one fine day in Chobe National Park.

This approach underscores what I call the Inverse Law of Wildlife Viewing: the fewer the number of gawkers, the greater the amount of wildlife you are likely to see and the more satisfying and uncompromised the experience.

In the course of several game drives conducted on board the Chobe Lodge's Unimog, I'd taken the time to strike up a closer acquaintance with a local Tswana guide named Patrick. Intercepting him on the grounds of the lodge a couple of days later, I inquired if he would be interested in taking the following day off to show me around. Just me. I would pay him for his services as well as for the use of one of the lodge's jeeps.

"Let me see what I can arrange." I could tell he was delighted by the offer, and I flatter myself that it was not just because of the extra money but also for a chance to take a break from his daily routine.

Having settled the necessary details with the management, we convened at first light the following morning. In the trees that surrounded the lodge, birds were singing loudly as they reacquainted themselves with the sun. Out front and in the wide, glassy gray river, hippos were snorting challenges like wrestlers working themselves up for a televised tag-team match. I stretched. The sun was barely up, and the air was almost cool. Patrick eyed me speculatively.

"Where do you want to go? What do you want to see?"

I gave him the same answer I give guides everywhere, from Ankara to

Alaska. "I want to go everywhere and see everything, but we only have one day. So you choose."

He smiled, nodded thoughtfully, and pointed to our waiting vehicle.

The jeep had no top and more interestingly, no doors, the better to allow for unobstructed game viewing. After a couple of hours spent paralleling the river and bouncing through dry forest, we eventually turned right and headed down toward the water. Within minutes, you could hardly see the forest for the elephants.

There were elephants everywhere. If you have only seen them in a zoo, you cannot imagine what it feels like to be virtually surrounded by elephants. As Tennyson might have put it, there were elephants to the right of us, elephants to the left of us, elephants in front of us. Yet in all this trunk-waving, dirt-kicking, lash-batting, throat-clearing throng, there was no chaos, no arguing, no confusion. Each herd or matriarch-led group stayed together. Despite what must have been a considerable collective thirst, there was no mad rush for the cool comfort and tipple of the river. One herd would remain at the edge of the forest, patiently cropping at what remained of the badly battered vegetation while waiting its turn at the water. Across an open, bare, gentle downward slope of compacted dirt and sand some eighty yards in extent, the members of another herd were wallowing in the mud, spraying one another with water, wrestling, and conversing as energetically and politely as a gaggle of soccer moms prior to their children's kickoff.

Off to one side, among the last line of trees and well away from the nearest of the waiting bathers, a single lioness lay on her belly and watched. Watched and waited as though she had all the time in the world.

From the front passenger seat of the open jeep, I stared in awe and amazement. I had seen more anarchy, disorganization, and hostility displayed at municipal swimming pools. I turned to Patrick. As I spoke, I gestured in the direction of the herd that was killing time at the forest's edge. Its nearest representative was taking a massive leak less than twenty yards from our vehicle.

"Why aren't those elephants heading down to the river?"

Patrick smiled knowingly. "It is not their time. Each herd will wait its turn so that a favorite wallowing place such as this does not become overcrowded."

Half an hour passed. The elephants that had been drinking and gamboling in the river began to vacate the beach and move out in the direction of the forest. As soon as they started up the slight slope, the herd that had been waiting at the forest's edge headed down. They passed one another like factory workers changing shifts. One particularly impressive female striding along less than a handful of yards from our jeep turned to glance at us as she headed for the water. Our eyes met. I received the distinct impression she would have liked to stop and chat except that she was thirsty and besides, in an hour or so, herd number three would be lining up to wait for their turn at the water, and she did not want to waste bathtime trying to make contact with yet another uncomprehending human.

I would have been satisfied to spend the remainder of the day there, watching elephants at play, rolling in the mud, marveling at how none of them stepped on the week-old baby frolicking without a care among tree-trunk-size legs. Instead, after forty minutes and a reluctant sigh, I signaled to Patrick that we should continue on upriver.

That was where, not too far inland at a place where gunmetal gray boulders flanked a small winding tributary of the Chobe, we came upon the devouring.

Lions working a fresh carcass are relentless in their single-minded ferocity. Unlike the jovial elephants that we had just left behind, nothing about the big cats' gritty activity smacked of playtime of any kind. For big cats, feeding is an ancient and bloody business that is pursued with deadly earnestness. A youngster attempting to force its way onto the corpse is liable to receive a punishing blow from a feeding male or mature female powerful enough to crush a human skull. The intimidating, bloodcurdling roars that periodically erupted from the heaving leonine mass contained none of the melancholy of the plaintive nocturnal bellowing my wife and I had heard at Tarangire.

When a lion looks up from a meal in progress, eyes wide, face and muzzle smeared from one side to the other with bright red blood and bits of torn flesh, it puts one in mind of something other than a child's smiling stuffed toy ready for nighttime cuddling. A feeding lion's appearance and attitude are as raw and intimidating as anything in nature.

Despite the gruesomeness of the scene, despite the ongoing carnage, I stared. You have no choice but to stare. It is impossible to turn away. A mass lion feed is exactly what one would see at a car accident if the rescue workers, instead of helping the injured victims, began to gnaw at their bodies.

"What are they eating?"

My voice had dropped to just above a whisper. It was an automatic, instinctive response to something sunk deep in my genes, a reaction to a more primeval time when keeping one's voice down in the presence of large carnivores was a matter not of politeness or custom but of life and death.

Patrick eyed the *grand guignol* with a professional squint. Though he must have come across similar displays of blood and bodily destruction many times, his expression was solemn. Unlike my voice, his did not change.

"Young elephant. Maybe five years old." Both hands resting on the top of the wheel, he sat up straighter in the driver's seat as he strained for a better look. "I don't think they killed it."

What? "Then how did it die?"

"Probably anthrax. Lots of anthrax in the park. Lions here don't have to hunt. They see a sick elephant, they just follow it until it falls over."

I had read that the lions of Chobe were among the biggest in the world. Now I understood one reason why. There was no shortage of food here, nor did hunting take a toll on their body mass. Feasting on dead elephants, the local cats had grown enormous.

Spine-chilling snarls continued to reverberate in the air as the members of the pride battled for the best spots, swarming the lifeless lumpy corpse like oversize piglets overwhelming a freshly filled trough. Intently seeking the slightest gap, impatient juveniles and cubs circled the impenetrable congregation of feeding adults. Black-tufted tails protruding from the tawny mass thrashed back and forth like the petals of wind-whipped flowers. Still sporting the camouflaging dark blotches of adolescence, one impatient male youngster passed the time until it would be his turn to eat by chasing off the vultures that had begun to gather on the fringes of the feed. *The King of the Beasts,* I thought as I smiled at his antics, albeit one with a very small "k."

I was unaware of how much time had passed until Patrick leaned toward me to murmur, "Enough?" I checked my watch and was surprised at the lateness of the hour. We had been watching the feeding lions from morning until well into midday. "What else would you like to see?"

I considered, then asked a question I often pose when traveling in the company of local people. "Where's *your* favorite place, Patrick? Not the lodge's—yours."

"Ah." His smile grew wide. "It's a bit of a drive from here. We may get back late, and no vehicles are supposed to be out in the park after dark."

I shrugged. "Blame me. Tell them the irritating American insisted, and you didn't want to be impolite."

He nodded, grinning, put the jeep in gear, and we continued westward upriver.

Coming upon the solitary lioness was an accident. Patrick had not been looking for her. Lolling on her stomach a few yards from the dirt track, head held high and paws stretched out in front of her, she was as elegant as a sphinx and nearly as motionless. She was lying on an open sandy patch with dense forest behind her and us and the river not far off to our left. For the first time since we had left the lodge, I was acutely conscious of the openness of the jeep, far more so than I had been among the elephants. Apprehensively, I searched the immediate surroundings, but to all intents and purposes she appeared to be alone.

Surprising me, Patrick cut the engine. This left me even more nervous, since engines take time to start. Relaxing in his seat, he put one foot up on the dash and leaned back. As far as I knew, there was no gun in the vehicle. Full-grown and magnificently muscled, the lioness barely acknowledged our presence. She was perhaps twenty feet away. The wonder and sheer magnificence of her proximity notwithstanding, I shamelessly found myself wishing that she had been taking her ease on the other side of the jeep—Patrick's side. That way, if she turned suddenly irritable, or hungry . . .

I glanced back at my guide. He looked completely at ease. *He knows these animals,* I reminded myself. *He lives among them, observes them daily, is knowledgeable about their habits, familiar with their moods, cognizant of their eccentricities. If he's not worried, can I be less?* I did note that, relaxed as he was, Patrick did not once take his eyes off the lioness. Unperturbed he might have been, but neither was he about to drift off to sleep.

I was very proud of myself for not saying anything. Perhaps he was waiting to see how I might react. If it was a test of some kind, I hope I passed. No doubt I'm overdramatizing the situation. Probably he just wanted me to have an experience I would remember.

On that account, he more than accomplished his goal.

"Is she sick?" On this occasion I felt no compunction about whispering. Once again, Patrick did not whisper, but he did keep his voice down for a change.

"I don't think so. Sometimes they just like to be by themselves, I think."

We watched her a while longer. I could have stayed there until night descended. She was so close, I could smell her. But while he was too polite to say so, I remembered Patrick's admonition that all vehicles had to be back at the lodge by sundown. I said nothing, just nodded that it was OK for us to go. He nodded back and reached for the ignition. As he did so, the lioness yawned.

I had seen lions yawn before and have seen them yawn since, but never so emphatically or at such close quarters. Eyes squeezed shut, she held her mouth open for a long time, revealing enormous canines white as kitchen porcelain, a long and perversely kittenish tongue, and healthy black gums. Her jaws and teeth looked capable of crunching rock, not to mention mere flesh and bone. She did not deign to look in our direction as we drove off.

In my life, I have seen many people and many animals open their mouths wide, but that solitary leonine gape on the south shore of the

Chobe remains to this day the most memorable yawn I have ever witnessed up close.

Patrick's favorite spot turned out to be a place where the Chobe River bends lazily to the north before swinging southeast, narrowing afresh, picking up speed, and resuming its churning rush toward the Zambezi River and *Mosi-oa-tunya*, the Tswana words for "The-Smoke-That-Thunders" (better known but not better enunciated as Victoria Falls). Below Patrick's bend, the water spreads out to give birth to numerous shallow sandbars that provide ideal habitat for wading birds and effortless haul-outs for basking crocodiles. Both were much in evidence when we arrived.

Parking as close to the shifting, car-trapping sands as we dared, we climbed out of the jeep and walked down to the water's edge. So shallow were the mirrorlike pools and shimmering capillaries of river that there was no place for a croc, much less an idling hippo, to hide. My knowledge of Botswanan ornithology being woefully defunct, I could only stare and marvel at the hundreds of shorebirds and other more infrequent avian visitors that flocked to the shallow plain to hunt and drink. Without having to ask, I immediately understood the reasons for my guide's affection for the place.

Setting directly behind the Chobe and somewhere over Namibia, the sun was dusting the water with tincture of sulfur and cinnabar. Walking farther out onto the crocodile-visited sands than I was willing to risk, Patrick stood with his hands on his hips silently admiring this small, secret corner of his homeland. For long moments, he forgot about me, and I was pleased to see him privately enjoying what so few others had the opportunity to share. I stood in silence on a slightly higher sandbar, my gaze shifting from the gold-suffused water to the wealth of animal life that was wholly intent on its sunset activity.

On another bank just in front of us, a small herd of impala was inspecting a solitary croc. One at a time, they would approach, sniff the motionless reptile, then apprehensively dart back out of reach. I thought their actions reckless and ignorant. But the cold-blooded croc was far more interested in soaking up the last warming rays of the setting sun than in helping itself to a dim-witted hors d'oeuvre.

Several puku, or Chobe bushbuck, wandered out of the woods to drink, their movements as delicate and coordinated as those of a string quartet playing Mozart. Chobe National Park is the only place in the world to see them, and I was conscious of the privilege. Perhaps it was the overriding tranquillity of the locale, but the animals and birds acted as if we were not present. Had we arrived in a growling dinosaurian Unimog sporting twenty chattering tourists, I suspect the unperturbed wildlife would have acted differently.

As he rejoined me, it was evident that Patrick had thoroughly enjoyed the respite from a day of having to explain to wide-eyed visitors why hippos are the most dangerous animals in Africa and that a water monitor is a spectacularly large lizard and not a gruff Afrikaner whose job it is to ensure the working of the lodge's hydraulic systems.

He glanced speculatively at the descending sun. "We're already late. We'll get back after dark."

I smiled. I had enjoyed every moment of the day, every second. "Like I told you, blame me. It's all my fault."

He nodded, smiling anew, as we climbed back into the jeep.

So used are most of us to city life that we have forgotten what real night is like. The all-encompassing darkness is accompanied by a multiplicity of sounds and noises that our ancestors made studious efforts to avoid. As we headed back toward the lodge, Patrick driving as fast as he dared along the dark dirt road, I could hear some of those primeval night noises even over the dogged grinding of the jeep's engine.

I was not worried about getting lost. Patrick had been a guide in the park for some time and knew all the dirt tracks intimately. Besides, with a major river always on our immediate left, it would be difficult to lose the way. His only real concern, other than the prospect of receiving a mild chewing-out from his supervisor for returning a guest well after dark, was the always-present chance of encountering elephants.

We were fifteen minutes from the lodge when he hung a sharp left at an intersection and followed it with a startled oath. I was thrown forward by the impact but managed to catch myself before my upper body could slam into the jeep's metal dash. My eyes fought to focus in the darkness.

In turning the corner, the jeep had not caught the couple in the twin beams of its headlights until it was too late. More than a little non-plussed, the female trotted hurriedly off to the right while her outraged mate nearly fell as he stumbled off in the opposite direction. I will never forget the look on that lion's face, so closely did his confusion, uncertainty, distress, and annoyance mimic that of a human male surprised in the same circumstance. Plainly, he was at that moment torn between a desire to slink off into the bush with his tail and everything else slunk between his legs and one that would see him leaping for the jeep with an eye toward ripping both of us to shreds.

To this day, I am not sure who was the more startled by the inadvertent collision, but I do know who was the most disappointed.

Giving the pair no time to decide what to do next, Patrick floored the accelerator and the jeep leaped forward, careening down the dirt road. Looking back, I could see only faint signs of the couple we had so rudely interrupted in the midst of their business. In another moment, they had been swallowed up by the African night.

I looked at Patrick. He looked at me. Then, despite ourselves, we both began to laugh. The jokes lasted all the way back to the lodge. Partly because such an encounter could not avoid engendering a certain amount of humor and partly because had any number of things gone wrong at the critical moment (the jeep overturning in the brush, or stalling out, or the lions reacting more quickly and antagonistically to our interruption) what had turned out to be merely amusing could have become deadly serious.

Back at the lodge, the two of us examined the front of the jeep. The glass over the left front headlight was cracked, and there was a small dent in the metal. Nothing major. I wondered if the lodge's insurance would cover it. Had the lions been humans, I have no doubt they would have filed suit. After bidding Patrick good night with a heartfelt "*Ke a leboga* or "thank you" (the only words I knew in Tswana), I retired to my room having acquired another bit of animal lore not generally to be found in the available handbooks.

Lions are especially aggressive at night, but if you happen to (literally) run into them when they are mating, I can say that their embarrassment seems equal to that of any human couple surprised under similar circumstances.

That's one day in the African bush. Travel agents will tell you that in order to see animals and experience a place you have to spend days there, or weeks. I have to disagree. As with anything else in life, quality trumps quantity. If you really want to experience the herd, blend with the herd, you have to find a way to get away from your own herd. The species people on a package tour end up seeing and hearing more than any other are the other people on the same package tour.

On that one day in Botswana, I saw common animals and rare animals, cooperation in drinking and bathing and cooperation in feeding. Life ending and life beginning. The circle of life is not a neat, perfect circle, but one that's cracked and distorted; frequently beautiful, sometimes ugly. But no matter what you're fortunate enough to see, whether the Dante-esque bacchanalia of a recent kill or the placid birdsong-scored tranquillity of an African sunset, it sure beats sitting in an office—or watching the same thing on TV.

XII

AIR JAWS

South Africa, June 2002

THE SKY OVER WESTERN CAPE had opened, and it was pouring down rain enough to sink a galleon. Except my friend Ron and I were not at sea. It only felt that way. Having left Augrabies Falls National Park in the province of Northern Cape, we had been driving all day in hopes of reaching Cape Town before dark. Heralded by mountainous dark clouds rolling up from Antarctica that concealed much of the region from sight, we had been driving through torrential rain for nearly an hour.

While I struggled to negotiate the alien streets in the dark and the rain, Ron poured over the map of the city and the instructions we had been sent. Either the hotel we had been told to stay at was not where it was supposed to be, we had been given inadequate directions, or the rain had swept us halfway to Durban. Nearly overcome by darkness and fatigue, we were ready to credit any of these possibilities.

"This is crazy," I finally muttered. "Forget the reservation. We know the boat leaves from Simon's Town. Lets go there and find a room."

Ron eyed me uncertainly. "Are you sure? You look pretty tired."

"I'm not tired; I'm exhausted. But I can find Simon's Town." As I was talking, I was trying to follow the highway signs. "We angle east around the main part of the city and then follow the roads south. If we reach the end of the continent, we've gone too far."

We eventually did arrive in Simon's Town, a quaint historical suburb of Cape Town that occupies part of a spaghettilike strip of land squeezed tightly between False Bay and the great hulking monolith that is Table Mountain. We also found, as we tried motel after motel, that there were no rooms to be had at the height of the storm. When we eventually did find a vacancy, it turned out to be nicer as well as more reasonably priced than any from which we had earlier been turned away. The fact that the South African Rand was about eleven to the U.S. dollar at that time boosted our spirits as well. Oblivious to hunger, the storm raging around us, and with poor prospects of seeing much of anything else that night, we collapsed gratefully onto our beds.

A cloud-streaked morning brought breakfast, conversation with the hotel's amiable and informative owner, gorgeous views out over the harbor and the bay, and the ironic news that by sheer fortuitous coincidence the boat on which we were to go out that morning just happened to leave from the dock at the base of the hotel. If we had found and stayed at the hotel back in Cape Town where a room had been reserved for us, we would have had to get back in our car and drive clear across town in order to embark on the next part of our journey. Having crapped out all the previous night, we had at the last moment and wholly through good luck inadvertently rolled a winner.

Maybe you've heard of Air Jaws, or seen the shows of that name on the Discovery Channel. In South Africa's False Bay, on the other side of the continental spine from the city of Cape Town, it was discovered some years ago that great white sharks regularly leap out of the water in pursuit of Cape fur seals, their favorite prey. It was there that Ron and I had decided to conclude our monthlong trek across the country in hopes of glimpsing this extraordinary predatory display.

Arrangements had been made in advance with Chris Fallows, the naturalist and photographer who had made the first serious studies of this remarkable behavior, to spend a couple of days with him and his fiancée (now wife) Monique as they pursued their efforts to document the sharks' activities. As with any animal behavior, we knew there was no guarantee we would see anything, even though it was the appropriate season for the sharks to be feeding.

I was prepared to be disappointed. In New Guinea, I once spent time at one of the world's foremost shore-diving facilities and saw practically nothing. Back in Port Moresby days later, my friend Dik Knight who owns Loloata Island Resort out in Bootless Bay informed me casually, "I know you had a bad time at Walindi. I just talked to them. This morning, their divers saw orcas and a sperm whale."

I believe my precise and carefully considered response to this was, "*Agghhh!*" Not an especially scientific reaction, but a sincere one.

If you go anywhere in the world *expecting* to see something and do not, it is understandable to be disappointed, but you must also be accepting. The natural world is not Disneyland, and the animals do not run on tracks.

The initial assessment we received was less than encouraging. Recent shark action at Chris's favored site, Seal Island, had been as sporadic and unpredictable as the weather. The second morning following our arrival at Simon's Town dawned chilly and damp, but by the time we set out, the worst of the weather had broken. The intermittent clouds suggested we might make it to the island without encountering any rain. In any event, Ron and I had come too far to be put off by the prospect of a little inclement weather. There was, however, one aspect of our incipient adventure I had not thought to discuss in advance.

I saw that Ron was eyeing Fallows's boat uncertainly. "You OK?" I asked him.

He nodded. "It's just that I get seasick sometimes."

Now he tells me. "I'm sure it'll be fine," I lied. "We'll be inside the bay at all times. It's not like we're going out on the open sea."

But, of course, we were. False Bay is huge, and completely open to the heaving, throbbing, great Southern Ocean.

The compact white cabin cruiser began to bounce and roll as Chris pulled away from the dock and gunned the engine. Ron immediately turned queasy and lurched toward a seat, but he handled his condition manfully. I'm not sure if he threw up on the way out to Seal Island or not. Having spent time around seasickness sufferers, I knew that the best one could do was leave them alone. It is of little use to ask someone who has turned green and is leaning over the side of a boat puking their guts out, "How are you feeling?" No matter how well intentioned, the attention is invariably not welcomed by the afflicted.

Sea the color of polished jade was churning to froth near the island itself where incoming Antarctic swells battered the bare rocks, but the sight of thousands of fur seals barking, arguing, nuzzling, and dropping in and out of the shallows was so engaging that Ron forgot he was supposed to be sick. The early morning clouds were now streaked a fiery red. As if in anticipation of what we had come hoping to see, the sky itself had been bloodied.

Chris and Monique had already apprised their passengers of what to look for. We had been joined for the day by a young couple and also by an American sound- and cameraman team who were shooting high-definition video for a nature film that had been commissioned by a wealthy Arab deeply interested in conservation. Familiar with the occupational travails nature photographers have to endure in their unending quest to get that special shot, I willingly yielded them the best viewing position on the boat's stern. Unlike their equipment, my handheld video camera was considerably more portable. In fact, it was smaller than most of their camera's lenses.

Every day in season the inhabitants of Seal Island perform the pinniped version of *High Noon,* except that it takes place early in the morning and late in the evening. The hungry seals know the sharks are out there, just offshore, gliding silently through the dark green water that surrounds the island. The hungry great whites know the seals are there, worrying themselves on the rocks, desperate to head out to their feeding grounds. The sharks are patient, the seals increasingly restless. Sooner or later every morning, a seal's hunger overcomes its caution, and it becomes the first of the herd to make a mad break for open water.

Within moments after the first brave island dweller has bolted for the blue, it seems as if the rocks themselves have been set in motion. Seals singly and in clusters avalanche into the sea. In less than a minute, the surface of the water is boiling with sleek bewhiskered shapes torpedoing at top speed for the feeding grounds of the southern Indian Ocean.

Below them, drawn upward by all the activity, the piscine equivalent of jet interceptors have begun to stir. Armed not with guns or missiles but with razor-sharp, serrated, triangular teeth set in multiple rows in jaws, the great whites begin working to single out potential victims. Ideally, they are looking for the younger, less experienced seals.

The deadly dance between predator and prey that takes place in False Bay perfectly exemplifies the great white's preferred method of attack. In this eternal ballet, the initial advantage goes to the seal. Great whites can strike with incredible speed and force, but they cannot turn as quickly as a seal. Think of a power lifter trying to catch a gymnast in a game of tag, or a battleship attempting to run down a PT boat. One has the advantage of overwhelming size and strength while the other is far more agile.

Seals know they are safe when they can see the shark. So great whites essentially mug their prey, coming up on them from below and behind. Just prior to the moment of impact, the shark's eyes roll back into its head. This is a protective reaction. Seals have big teeth and sharp claws. Like a raptor smashing talon-first into the spine of a rabbit, the shock of a great white's initial strike is often enough to kill. In False Bay, this hit is also delivered with enough force to not only drive the prey completely upward out of the water, but to send the shark airborne along with it. Hence the name Air Jaws that has been applied to the hunting great whites in this part of the world.

But where to look to see the phenomenon, and how to observe a behavior that is as transitory as it is fantastic?

"Keep your attention near the horizon," we were told. All very well and good, but drifting in a small boat in the middle of an enormous bay one sees an awful lot of horizon. We drifted and stared, stared and nibbled snacks. With each passing moment, the parade of departing seals moved farther and farther out to sea. Soon the island would be bereft of all but the youngest pups.

"There!"

At Monique's excited shout, I turned sharply to my right. Off in the distance, a large gray-white shape was just falling back into the water. There was no mistaking the cause. A great white had taken a seal and having breached, was falling back into the water on its left side. The entire episode occupied a second, maybe two, of astonished time. Then, just like that, it was over. Eyes alight, adrenaline pumping, I looked over at Ron.

"Well, we got to see it, anyway."

The only flush to his face came from the cold. Dejectedly, he held up a half-consumed muffin. "I was eating. I missed it."

I felt terrible for him. Having come all this way, the long drive, the cold and soggy night—it just wasn't fair. But that's wildlife viewing. It never is fair or reasonable. A certain Australian tiger shark as silent as it was contemplative could attest to that.

The morning, however, was far from over, and our hosts had a surprise in store. I don't know if they employ it on every trip, but they had a reputation to uphold, and they were not about to let a professional film crew depart without helping them to acquire the best footage possible. In the course of their extensive studies of great white shark behavior, Chris and Monique have developed a method of, if not ensuring a good shot or two, at least greatly improving the odds on behalf of the photographer.

In making their attack from behind and below, great whites rely on their excellent vision. Unable to catch a sprightly, far more nimble seal that's able to turn on a sand dollar and dart off in any of three dimensions, they search for one that's swimming or resting on the surface. This is a principal reason why surfers are sometimes attacked. From below, especially in murky water, a surfer or especially a boogie boarder sitting on his board with his legs and arms dangling over the side looks remarkably like the silhouette of a seal. A slick black wet suit only enhances the illusion. It's why surfers who have been attacked by great whites speak of being literally thrown out of the water. Mistaken for seals, they've been struck from below.

Keen to avoid a seal's thrashing teeth and flailing claws, a great white will often strike, bite, and then back off, circling a short safe distance away while it waits for its prey to expire from shock and loss of blood. This behavior is what allows many surfers who have been hit to survive—provided the shark's initial attack takes a bigger bite out of their fiberglass board than their torso or limbs. No such option is available to the seal. A deep wound to the body almost invariably leads to death, though if the first bite is shallow or glancing, or primarily takes a piece of tail or flipper, the seal sometimes survives.

Later that morning, we encountered the victim of one such slipshod assault. Right flipper dangling, trailing blood through the water, it was fighting to make it back to the island. All of us on board followed its progress with a mixture of fascination and trepidation. All that blood—there seemed no way the seal, painfully working its way along the surface with only one functional flipper, could escape the notice of the patrolling sharks.

No matter how jaded one is to the indifference of Nature in the wild, no matter how many kills one has witnessed or come across, as humans, it is impossible to look upon such a scene without becoming at least somewhat emotionally involved. We found ourselves rooting for the seal until it was safely back in the shallows that surround the island.

I looked at Chris. "Do you think it'll live?"

He pondered. "It lost a lot of blood, and I don't see how that flipper can heal. But believe it or not, we've seen seals on the island with worse injuries and they seem healthy enough." He smiled slightly. "So yes, it's possible."

Then he turned away, moved to the stern, and began to put out the surprise.

Cut from a piece of black neoprene, the decoy was life-size. No professional sculptor would have admitted authorship of the crude lure, but Monique assured me it had proven quite effective. The rubbery seal silhouette was tossed off the back of the boat and the line attached to its nose carefully played out. Soon it was bobbing along behind us, easily cresting the small waves stirred up by our wake. At a distance of ten yards or so, it didn't look very realistic to me. I wondered what it must look like from below.

Chris headed the boat away from the island. Turning to Monique, I'm sure the reservations I was having must have crept into my voice.

"This works?"

"Not every time," she admitted. "The sharks have to be in the mood, active, and hungry enough to bite." She nodded sternward. "Just watch the decoy—and cross your fingers."

I considered. "How often do you have to replace the decoy?"

"A few times each season." She shrugged. "It can get pretty torn up."

Her instructions were simple enough. Except that while they explained how we were to *look* for a striking shark, they failed to explain how we were supposed to *photograph* it. At least, I had a video camera. Even assuming the decoy did its job, to get a decent still picture of such abrupt, fast-moving, quickly-over-and-done-with action demanded the best efforts of the world's most skilled wildlife photographers—such as David Doubilet and Amos Nachoum, both of whom owe their classic shots of leaping great whites to the shark-finding skills of Chris and Monique Fallows.

I'm no David Doubilet or Amos Nachoum. All I could do was point the camera in the direction of the decoy, let it run, and cross my fingers—no, couldn't do that, because I had to hold and position the camera. Off to one side, Ron clutched his still camera and joined me in watching and waiting. So did the professional film team, who despite their thousands of dollars' worth of equipment could do no better than sit and stare and wait together with the rest of us.

Time slogged onward. Though I feared setting my camera aside at just the wrong moment, I had no choice but to rest my hands and arms from time to time. I shot interminable footage of a piece of scissored neoprene banging and bouncing along behind the boat. I acquired excellent images of the occasional patrolling seabird. I . . .

The water erupted behind the boat.

With the decoy clamped in its jaws and its head and upper body facing toward us, the enormous great white came completely out of the water before slamming back in on its right side. It looked more like a whale breaching than a fish jumping. White water geysered in every direction as it smashed back into our wake. The noise of the colossal splash reached us even above the deep-throated hum of the boat's engines. I gaped at the now calm patch of ocean that had been so briefly but violently shattered by the impossible leap. Had I actually seen what had just happened, or had I imagined it?

Standing nearby, Monique helpfully reconfirmed the stunning reality that had just transpired in front of me. "Did you get it?" she asked me when the cheering on the boat finally died down.

"What?" I turned to face her.

"Did you get it?" She indicated my camera. "The picture?"

I didn't know. Retiring to the shelter of the boat's small cabin, I rewound the tape. And there it was. It looked utterly unreal, as if I had imported a few seconds of footage from a television documentary. But I had indeed just seen a great white shark go completely airborne directly aft of the very boat on which I was still a passenger.

Subsequent to that one instant of experiencing Nature at her most spectacular, Ron and I would happily have returned to Simon's Town, concluding our monthlong visit to South Africa on a note as high as any wildlife enthusiast could desire. Now that we had been granted the privilege of beholding a sight seen by only a few, we allowed ourselves to relax. If we saw another attack and breach, all well and good. It would count as a bonus. If not, well, we considered ourselves content. I had seen, with my own eyes, an airborne great white. I picked up a muffin.

Not even Chris or Monique could have predicted what happened next.

Like everyone else on board, I continued to watch the decoy. Occasionally, I would let the camera run, capturing yet more endless dull footage of dark water and our V-shaped wake. From time to time, I would take a bite of muffin or chew on a mouthful of crackers. The air was clammy and chill, but the cloud cover had finally broken for good. Above the bay, patches of blue sky struggled to assert themselves.

It is the times when Providence is not called upon that it often chooses to manifest itself most forcefully. I just happened to have the camera running.

I heard Monique let out an "Oh, my God!" This from Monique Fallows, who every year spends months at a time in the company of sharks, and whom you'd think would be jaded. There were gasps from the others on board.

Directly behind us, fifteen feet and more than a ton of great white had launched itself from the depths. Shooting straight up with the decoy in its mouth, it rose out of the water like a Polaris missile, seemed to hang motionless for a moment, and then did a complete flip before returning to the sea snout-first. It was the kind of jump a big game fish like a marlin might make—not a great white shark. I lowered my camera. As I did so, I happened to catch the eye of the visiting cinematographer.

Though from the time we had left the dock he had been genial enough, we had exchanged little in the way of conversation. He was on assignment, had work to do, and was understandably more involved with his equipment than his fellow passengers. It occurred to me that this was the first time I had actually seen him smile. And a wide smile it was, too.

"Got it?" I asked hopefully, echoing Monique.

He nodded. His tone was restrained, but he was unable to keep the elation from his voice. "Got it."

So had I, with my little hand-held consumer video camera. It is a wonderful thing to be able to freeze-frame such a sequence, to see a great white shark suspended in the air, completely out of the water, with its snout pointed straight down and its tail flailing at the heavens. I have no doubt a panel of diving judges would card it a ten across the board.

We had one more breach on the decoy that morning. I had deliberately set my camera aside, wanting to experience, to remember this remarkable sight without viewing it through a lens. The shark came at the decoy from an angle more shallow than its predecessors, snapped it up in its mouth, and for an instant was also completely out of the water, its belly and underside perfectly parallel to the surface and its snout pointed toward our stern. It looked as if we were being pursued by some lethal low-flying aircraft. When the shark splashed back down with the decoy, its visit became the third close breach of the day, including that astounding

360-degree leap. As a coda, on the way back to Simon's Town, we came upon a pod of romping minke whales.

That particular day, by any standard, had turned out to be something much more than ordinary.

XIII

DRACULA IS A MUTE

Northern Borneo, September 2010

AN EFFICIENT VAMPIRE NEVER WAKES its victim, never unsettles their sleep, never alerts them to its bloodsucking presence, for the very good reason that the meal in question might object to serving as someone else's dinner. Whether the fabled count himself injected anesthetic into his quarry in the course of his nocturnal imbibitions is a subject that never seems to merit discussion in the innumerable films in which he has starred. Similarly, the matter of whether or not his saliva included a useful dose of anticoagulant to keep the blood flowing freely is also glossed over. The producers of such entertainments would rather focus on cleavage than coagulants.

In real life, those that thrive by drinking the blood of another usually, but not always, possess both weapons to facilitate their dining. Being subject to the attentions of one in particular turned out to be an oddly neutral experience. Not that it's one I'd care to repeat, even for demonstration purposes. Still, I couldn't escape the feeling afterward that the simple yet supremely efficient animal that had partaken uninvited of my bodily fluids was somehow apologetic regarding the entire incident.

I've mentioned my brief encounter with a single leech in Papua New Guinea. It was small and so was its appetite. The tiger leech is another matter entirely: one that I unwillingly encountered in the Danum Valley of northern Borneo.

The Danum is protected primary rain forest. Having never been cut, it's still densely populated with exotic creatures such as pangolins, binturongs, flying frogs and squirrels, five feline species, including the rarely seen clouded leopard, the even rarer Sumatran rhino, pygmy elephants, many primate species besides the iconic orangutan, insects that look as if they were designed by Fabergé, and leeches. Millions and millions of leeches. No matter how hard you try to avoid them, they . . . will . . . find . . . you.

While the common brown leech of Borneo (length less than two inches) tends to hug the rain-forest floor, the much larger tiger leech prefers to hang out on the ends of branches and leaves waiting for potential hosts to amble by. Able to sense its prey by both movement and heat, it will extend itself to its full length from the very tips of leaves in hopes of latching on to a passing meal. Once on board, it will efficiently and with surprising speed seek out bare flesh, attach its mouthparts, and begin to feed.

I got struck twice, and both times if was my fault. The first occasion can be attributed to hubris, the second to oversight.

My choice of jungle gear is a pair of long pants and a long-sleeved shirt made by the now sadly vanished firm of Willis & Geiger. W & G was bought by a much larger firm that, in the daffy pseudo-prescient manner of such companies, decided the market for such specialized gear did not justify the cost of producing it. In all the years I've worn this carefully preserved clothing, nothing has ever managed to bite or sting through it. Not an army ant, not a wasp, nothing.

Preparing to set out on a hike upriver, I carefully checked my attire. Long-sleeved shirt tucked into belted pants. Hiking socks and hiking boots. Broad-brimmed hat intended not to keep off the rain or sun so much as to provide a barrier against Things That Drop Out of Trees. All gear prepped and sprayed with permethrin. Insect repellent lightly slathered on exposed hands, face, and neck. And as the final touch, leech socks especially acquired for walking in the Danum. Unlike your standard hiking socks, whose breathable weave leeches can easily penetrate, leech socks are fashioned of fabric impervious to their probing. Something like plastic bags for your feet and lower legs, they are tied below the knee and add virtually no weight to your trek.

Thus equipped and having already successfully concluded several walks in the forest without having received so much as a single nibble, I felt perfectly safe in setting out once again.

The humidity that morning was high even for the Danum, and as the day warmed, I began to perspire more than usual. Long before I reached the end of the trail, I was steamed and drenched. At the terminus of this particular hike lies a flat, triangular peninsula of water-tumbled stone that sticks like a stony tongue out into the Danum River. Worn smooth by centuries of flash floods, car-size boulders dot the rubble-strewn terrain. The cooling breeze blowing down the river proved irresistible.

After carefully checking one especially inviting, smooth-topped boulder to ensure it was uninhabited, I removed my shirt and lay down to cool off. Ten delightful minutes later, I sat up and happened to catch a glimpse of my nether regions.

My legs were crawling with leeches.

Brown and tiger, they were inching their way upward like miniature malevolent Slinkies in search of exposed flesh. They were unable to live in the water and unable to live on the hot rocks, but they were perfectly comfortable lying dormant in the moist sand and mud while waiting for a mouse deer, a bearded pig, or an overconfident visitor like myself. Keeping as calm as I could, I first checked my exposed chest. Thankfully finding nothing, I returned my attention to my legs and began to flick the ravenous visitors away. Except, they didn't flick. Hanging on with ferocious single-mindedness, they forced me to pick them off one by one, roll them up, and toss them aside.

I made a thorough job of it, checking and rechecking to ensure that not a single one had escaped my notice and trying not to think about what would have happened had I chanced to fall asleep on that fine, cool, comforting rock. One or two leech bites are harmless enough. Several would be more than a little uncomfortable. The potential effects on the body of several dozen gorging themselves when combined with the hot tropical sun and humidity was one I chose not to contemplate.

Satisfied that I had seen off the last of them, I put my shirt back on, tucked it back in, and started back toward the trailhead. Looking down as I left, I saw still more of the hungry worm-shapes looping in my direction. I did not exactly sneer as I left them lurching futilely in my wake, but I did feel undeniably superior. With a single stride, I could cover more ground than any leech could in many minutes of extending itself to the fullest.

Hubris. A bad companion in the jungle.

Well pleased with myself and having thoroughly enjoyed the morning's outing, I returned to my room at the lodge and immediately began to remove my sopping wet clothing in anticipation of the refreshing shower to come. Shoes, leech socks, and hiking socks came off outside, then the rest inside. I pulled off my shirt and prepared to hang it over the back of a chair to dry and . . .

Plop.

Plop is a sound more frequently associated with cartoon audio effects than real life, but I can assure you that what I heard at that moment was inarguably a distinct *plop*. Frowning, I looked around and down. Lying on the floor was an oblong shape about as long and thick as my thumb. It was a dark red-brown in color and quivering ever so slightly. Bending, I took a closer look. It was a tiger leech, and it was quivering because it was full of me.

I don't care what people say about maintaining scientific detachment. Unless they are your specialty, parasites are an unpleasant sight at any time. Seeing one lying on the floor bloated with an ounce or two of your own blood and writhing drunkenly in a desperate but feeble attempt to get away produces sensations in mind and gut that are anything but dispassionate.

Resisting the urge to stomp my attacker to a pulp (and not wanting to mess the hardwood floor), I fought back the urge to heave, carefully scooped him up, and dumped him over the porch railing. There was nothing to be gained by artificially bringing forward the creature's demise, besides which, birds and other creatures feed on leeches and might find this overstuffed individual especially nourishing. Feeling not very circle-of-life–ish, I stripped off the rest of my clothes and headed for the shower, wondering where and how I had been bitten.

The answer to both questions was soon forthcoming. Just above the waistband of where my pants snugged against my body, a perfectly circular wound not much smaller than a dime was bleeding merrily away. I immediately cleaned it with soap and water. It continued to bleed. I patted it down and put pressure on it with a clean towel. As soon as I moved the towel away, the bleeding resumed. I put a Band-Aid over it. It bled through the Band-Aid. There was absolutely no pain or discomfort. Just a steady flow of crimson me.

Digging into my supplies, I pulled out a packet of QR powder. Originally intended for the military, it's formulated to instantly stop the bleeding from any wound. I was gratified to discover that it also works on tiger leech bites. But only temporarily. As long as the leech's anticoagulant enzyme hirudin remains active in the wound, it will continue to bleed. Once my QR-induced scab came off, the bleeding resumed, albeit at a slower flow.

This is not dangerous, but it plays hell with your laundry.

Unlike the brown leech, which adds an anesthetic to the mix, the bite of the tiger leech is a sharp pinch you can feel. The one that got me must have hidden in the folds of my shirt, waiting to bite me until I put it back on. For such a primitive creature, it's a sneaky little bastard. I felt the pinch, but thought it was from my waistband being too tight when I'd put my shirt back on.

The second time I got bit was on the drive out of the Danum and back to the base town of Lahad Datu. Anticipating no reason to get out of the 4x4, I was wearing much more comfortable attire: shorts and a slightly undersized sleeveless shirt. On the way out, however, the driver stopped the vehicle and gestured at the top of a nearby tree.

"Crested serpent eagle," he explained, believing I'd want to get a picture. Indeed, I did. So I climbed out, camera in hand, and approached the tree for a better view, being careful of course not to make contact with any of the vegetation.

But you don't have to make contact with the vegetation. Sensing you coming, the tiger leech can extend its body two or three inches outward over empty space. As I discovered later that night, this was more than enough to reach me.

Unlike my previous passenger, I never saw this one. Doubtless sated and content, it dropped off somewhere between the towns of Lahad Datu and Semporna. The calling card it left behind was unmistakable, though. That evening when I removed my shorts in the hotel, more than half a foot of fabric along the waistband was stained red. That's right; I had been bitten in the same latitude, only this time five inches closer to my navel. They don't hesitate, tiger leeches. Finding unprotected flesh, they immediately dig in and suck away.

Whereas brown leech bites fade with time, tiger leech bites sometimes leave permanent marks. I still have both of mine. More irritating is the fact that even after three trips through the system, my dry cleaner is unable to extirpate all of the bloodstains on my irreplaceable trekking clothes. Whenever that bothers me too much, however, I just think back to that lazy morning on the Danum River shore, and what might have happened had I decided to drift off into a long, quiet nap instead of rousing myself and moving on. Who knows?

I might still be drifting.

XIV

TEENAGE KILLER NINJA OTTERS

Southwestern Brazil, May 2000

OVER THE YEARS, I'VE BEEN fortunate enough to have observed and had encounters in the wild with hundreds of different animals. Big animals, small animals, animals considered conventionally beautiful, and animals regarded as unattractive. Creatures of the air, sea, and land. Some too small to see without the aid of a magnifying glass and others too big to avoid. Animals so inoffensive they would not harm you no matter how loutishly you intruded on their space, and animals of fallaciously benevolent mien that would chew your toes off entirely unprovoked.

From among this raging, mewling, bellowing, snorting, stridulating menagerie, I am often asked, "Which is your favorite?"

Well, if I had to choose one . . .

It is a predator, though at first glance you might not think of it as such. If you have never been fortunate enough to come across an otter in person, you've certainly seen them on television. Otters have served as the stars of innumerable nature documentaries. Among all the denizens of the animal kingdom, few possess such natural magnetism or seem to have as much actual *fun* as the otter; rocketing effortlessly through the water, tobogganing headfirst down snowbanks, playing frenetic king-of-the-mountain atop slick rocks or convenient logs. Through no design of their own, otters fit comfortably into that non-Linnaean but very real and entirely human-created genus known as *Cute*. Not only are they naturally playful, they are furry, inoffensively small, bewhiskered, family-oriented, and they squeak charmingly. Note that the actual differences from rats, about which most people feel quite differently, are comparatively minor.

As I have already pointed out, we are an incorrigibly visual species.

There is one kind of otter, however, that while possessing in full all of the aforementioned Lutrinaean characteristics can be something less than playful and react in a manner other than cute. It is my favorite predator as well as my favorite animal in the world.

Pteronura brasiliensis, the giant otter of South America, can grow to more than six feet in length and attain a weight of nearly eighty pounds. Cross your prototypical cuddly river otter with a seal and you'll get some idea of what this master of the Amazon basin looks like out of the water. The giant otter is the largest member of the weasel family. In Spanish, it is known as *el lobo de río* or "the river wolf." An apt name for a predator that eats piranhas for breakfast, along with pretty much anything else it can catch. Every bit as agile in the water as its smaller cousins, it is able to consume much larger prey.

Excluding humans, the giant otter's only real enemy is the caiman, particularly the black caiman. From its massive snout to its spiky dragon's tail, this striking South American crocodilian can reach lengths of twenty feet. Individually, a giant otter is easy prey for the caiman. But a cooperative family group of otters cannot only drive off the armored giants, they have been known to kill smaller ones.

They have also been reputed, on rare occasions, to seriously injure humans who intrude on their territory.

Nearly wiped out by decades of uncontrolled hunting for their pelts, giant otters are now protected in many parts of the continent. Where their habitat has been left intact, they are making a slow but steady comeback from near extinction. Endangered but viable populations are reported from Guyana, Brazil, Peru, Ecuador, and Bolivia. Despite their wide range they remain scarce and often difficult to see. Though I missed them in Guyana, I have been fortunate enough to encounter them while crossing the small lakes they favor in Peru, Ecuador, and Brazil. From the time I first learned of their existence, it became a dream of mine to interact with them in their natural surroundings. In other words, to go swimming with them.

Knowledgeable people to whom I confessed this longing told me in no uncertain terms that in their professional opinion this was a Really Bad Idea. Not unlike scratching a cheetah between its front legs.

"A family group will almost always include one or two cubs, or at least juveniles, and they're highly protective of their young," one zoologist explained to me when I broached the possibility.

I nodded understandingly. "So if I just happened to find myself in the water in their vicinity, what would they be likely to do?"

The specialist considered. "One of three things. They'll swim away, in which case you're wasting your time. They'll hang around briefly to satisfy their curiosity, barking and spy-hopping (lifting themselves vertically out of the water to get a better view of their immediate surroundings), in which case you'll get a nice photo-op. Or they'll attack, in which case you are frankly putting your life at risk."

I smiled wanly. "Maybe they'd just give me a warning nip to drive me out of the water."

My friend stared hard me. "Maybe. Or maybe they'll snap an arm, or bite off part of your hand. They eat bones, you know. If you're not close to land or a boat and they take a couple of good chunks out of you, that'll put a lot of blood in the water real fast. Which alters the environment in ways you don't want it to be altered."

I knew where he was heading. "Piranha," I said. He nodded solemnly.

This florid conversational caveat was at the forefront of my thoughts as I left my motel room and made my way to the small dock. Located on the side of the two-lane Transpantaneira highway that runs from the Brazilian city of Cuiabá to its terminus at the town of Porto Joffre in the heart of the Brazilian Pantanal, the Best Western Mato Grosso (yes, there really is such a place) was the only real hotel in the vast swampy region. The size of France, the Pantanal is the world's largest wetland. While most of it lies within Brazil, significant portions extend into Bolivia and Paraguay. A paradise for wildlife of all kinds, it is under threat from expanding agricultural development and from proposals to alter the main river system into which it drains.

The portion of the Pixaim ("pee-zham") River I was about to explore was human inhabited, but save for the occasional incursion by herds of cattle it had suffered relatively little degradation from commercial exploitation. White caimans lay like chevrons on both dusty brown banks, occasionally hauling themselves up onto the boat ramps to sun themselves. Jabirus, storks that can be as tall as people, wandered along the shore like so many hopeful undertakers, careful to stay just out of snapping range of the motionless but ever-watchful crocodilians. Southern caracaras marched up and down the dock area and the rest of the modest hotel grounds, looking for handouts.

These bold, handsome, chicken-size, land-loving predatory birds quickly lose their fear of humans and will allow you to approach quite close. While they will take live prey, they prefer carrion. They were also more than willing, I discovered, to sneak into the hotel's restaurant via its unscreened windows to scour unguarded plates of everything from bacon scraps to scrambled eggs and toast. Striding purposefully about the grounds as if they own the place, they remind anyone with an interest in paleontology of the great carnivorous flightless birds such as *Phororhacos* and *Diatryma* that used to roam these very same savannas not so many millennia ago.

Making inquiries soon after our arrival, my friend and I had been told that one or two families of giant otters had recently been spotted upriver. Conditions for a search were perfect. Though humid as always, the weather was unusually cool, in the seventies, and the forecast called for continued clear skies.

Heading up the Pixaim at first light the following morning, we encountered herds of capybaras almost immediately after setting out. Groups of the world's largest rodent grudgingly made way for our small aluminum skiff. A South American native that is most assuredly *not* in danger of extinction, capybaras are as prolific as any of their much smaller relations. They are also reputed to be good eating, though I have somehow missed every opportunity to find out for myself. More than anything, they look and act like giant semiaquatic guinea pigs. Grunting as they alerted one other of our approach and shaking the water from their thick brown fur, they would scramble on their stubby legs up onto one bank or the other and cluster there to observe our passage.

The Pantanal is an Eden for birds, especially for water birds. In addition to both jabirus and wood storks, as we continued upriver we recorded brown ibises, egrets, and white-throated herons. Red-crested cardinals flashed crimson against blue sky while white-necked kingfishers seemed to occupy every other tree branch overhanging the narrow river. Turquoise-throated parrots took pride in periodically shattering the silence with their raucous cries. Overhead, a single black cacique performed aerial acrobatics in the course of its search for prey. Meanwhile clusters of six- to eight-foot-long white caimans sunned themselves on the banks. Watching them, I was mindful of the secret desire I had not revealed to my traveling companion Gil or to our boatman.

But where were the otters? Atypically "cool" weather or not, it was plenty hot in the open metal boat. We slugged down liters of water and promptly sweated it all back out.

Each bend in the river exposed one wonderful new sight after another. A rookery tree growing right at the water's edge was home to more than a thousand snowy egrets. Several brilliantly dark blue hyacinth macaws, the largest member of the parrot family, soared past on three-foot wings, their presence belying their highly-endangered status throughout their range.

As I leaned to my left to peer over the side of the speeding boat, I reflected that there might be a dozen giant otters swimming along just beneath our keel and we would be utterly unaware of their presence. Like so many South American streams, the Pixaim was a blackwater river. Blackwater rivers are known as such because they are suffused with tannin, a substance produced by decaying vegetation that turns the water dark. The upper reaches of such rivers have the color of iced tea or Coca-Cola. In fact, tannins are present in strong tea, as well as in red wine and certain fruits. Cruising along a river rich in tannins, it is impossible to see more than a foot down into the depths.

Most of the morning had passed when eventually we turned yet another bend in the river and found ourselves confronted by a small boat. Its bow and stern were occupied by swarthy men wielding long cane poles. They might have been fishermen anywhere in the world save for their catch, which consisted of several exotic catfish and some two dozen piranhas. Piranhas, by the way, are quite tasty. Lots of small bones, and they taste a lot like trout. Best when pan-fried in butter, with salt and pepper to taste.

Had they seen any otters? After motoring upriver all morning, we were not sanguine. Raising an arm, the man in the bow pointed straight ahead and replied in Portuguese. Knowing only a few words of the local language, I turned questioningly to my guide and friend.

Gil was looking past me. "He says they're right over there, in the reeds."

I whirled. So as not to frighten away the fishermen's quarry, our boatman had cut our engine when we had drawn near. We were drifting forward with the slight current—and in the right direction.

Searching for the lean, hydrodynamic shapes I had seen before in oxbow lakes in Peru, at first I could see nothing but murky water and thick green growth. Then, there it was: an almost doglike head atop a body covered in short golden-brown fur splotched with decorative white on the neck and chest. The watchful, intelligent eyes turned speculatively toward us as their owner bobbed vertically up and down in the water, spy-hopping. Diving and then reappearing, several otters were working their way through the reed bed where they were hunting. I spotted another, and then another. There were perhaps half a dozen—definitely a family group or part of a larger one.

We had been sitting in silence and delighting in their antics for maybe ten minutes when Gil, who had been chatting as softly as possible with the fishermen, whispered to me, "They say this group will take fish from them, but only if it's really fresh. Will you buy a piranha?"

My expression must have been glowing. I replied positively.

By tossing bits of fresh-cut piranha into the water in our direction, the fishermen managed to coax several of the otters closer to our boat. One especially bold individual came right up alongside, rearing a foot or more of its muscular body up above the surface and chirping at us for all the world like a puppy begging for a biscuit. Once when it came particularly close, I cautiously reached out toward the giant otter. It drew back about a foot before lurching sharply up and forward again. Having over the years grown more than a little fond of my fingers, and needing all of them in order to type efficiently, I quickly pulled my hand back.

Below the surface in a tannin-obscured river, what would wriggling human fingers look like to a giant otter? Alien primate digits—or tempting small fish? I resolved to keep my fingers pressed together as much as possible while I was treading water. Because I had every intention of going in.

I turned to Gil. "Ask them if any of them have ever tried to go swimming with the otters."

The response to my inquiry was immediate and succinct. "They say they don't know of anybody who has tried it."

I debated with myself. "What do they think of the idea?"

Once more, Gil queried the fishermen. I saw one of them smile and shrug. "They say you can do whatever you want."

Not much help there. But nothing especially discouraging, either. Nothing along the lines of, "You can do whatever you want, but last week the otters ate my cousin's sister."

At such decisive moments in life, one often finds oneself not only isolated in intention, but in information. I had nothing to guide me; there was little in the available literature about the pros and cons of actually swimming with *Pteronura brasiliensis*. Now, confronted with the actual opportunity to do so, there was even less. I knew that people had interacted safely with giant otters they had rescued, and Cousteau *père* infamously had one aboard his ship during the filming of his Amazon adventure. But these were wild otters. They were not orphaned cubs that had been raised by surrogate human parents, and they were not injured animals that had been devotedly nursed back to health. They were entirely undomesticated.

But this family group had become at least partially habituated to a human presence due to being fed by the local fishermen. As long as they didn't mistake any wavering parts of me for a choice bit of filleted piranha, I should be all right. At least, that was what I told myself. Repeatedly. My concern at the prospect of being bitten was not the damage that might result from a bite itself, but the possible reaction of other hungry dwellers in the depths of the Pixaim that might be attracted to any such inadvertent bloody offering.

Do this, I told myself, *or go home and forever wonder what might have been.*

I started to slip out of my shirt and shorts. Underneath, I had worn a swimsuit in anticipation and in hope of being able to fulfill my long-held dream. Now that I was confronted with the reality, however, I found myself moving much more slowly. It wasn't the prospect of possible hostility on the part of the otters that held me back. It was not even the undeniable presence of piranhas in the river as confirmed by the fishermen's catch. It was the river itself. Because of the tannins, I would be lucky to be able to see my submerged hand in front of me once I was immersed in the shadowy water.

Gil was watching me carefully. "Are you sure you want to do this?"

I nodded. "I want to. I have to."

He said nothing more. Neither did our boatman. Seeing me stripped down to my swimsuit but still lingering in the skiff, the two fishermen were looking at me and murmuring among themselves. *How could I back out now?* I asked myself. *I'd look like a fine idiot in front of these two men.* I had no choice. By revealing my swimsuit I had committed myself. Or might find myself committed, when I got back home to tell the story. *If* I got back home to tell the story.

Although our little outboard was small, it suddenly seemed an amazingly long way over the side and down to the water. There was, of course, no ladder. Bare feet first, I slipped myself over the gunwale. The silvery metal was as hot against my belly and chest as the water crawling up my legs was cool. I would readily have enjoyed a swim if I had not been so uncertain as to the nature of my fellow swimmers. Hanging on to the side with both hands, ready to pull myself back into the boat at a moment's notice, I looked around anxiously, not nearly as cool as the water in which I was presently submerged. Viewed from eye level, the river in which I now found myself looked even darker. Blackwater, indeed. I could see into it to a depth of about six inches. Below that, all was chilly, wet, absolute gloom. What was swimming around down there, out of view and just under my feet? What might have been attracted by the disturbance of my entry? I had no idea how deep the river was at this place.

Nothing nibbled my toes. A curious caiman would most likely approach on the surface and could be spotted by those around me. I had the benefit of four lookouts on two boats. But I continued to hang onto the side, unwilling as yet to abandon the safety offered by the skiff.

I looked up at Gil. "Can you see them? Where are they?"

He shook his head. "I think maybe they went away when you entered the water."

All this preparation, all this mental anguish, I thought, *for nothing?* A part of me was relieved—but the other, the larger part, was crushed. I was on the verge of climbing back into the boat when Gil unexpectedly and with a tinge of excitement in his voice announced, "No, one is still here."

I spun around in the water, one hand gripping the gunwale tightly. I could feel the strain in my arm. "Where?" My eyes practically level with the surface, I couldn't see a damn thing.

Gil pointed. "Over there. It's coming straight toward you!"

I whirled, swirling water around me. Nothing. I couldn't see anything in the river.

"It just went down," Gil alerted me.

Something struck my right thigh. Reflexively, I jerked upward. Gil's tone was suddenly anxious.

"It bite you?"

"No." I took careful stock of my leg and its immediate vicinity. "No.

Just bumped me." I noticed that Gil was staring straight down as he activated the video camera. Delight replaced concern in his voice.

"I can see it clearly. It's right next to you. This is wonderful!"

I looked around; I looked down. I couldn't . . . see . . . anything. My frustration knew no bounds. "Where?" I pleaded. "Where *is* it?"

"Right beside you—oh, it's gone now."

I slowed my frantic turning. Evidently I had been the recipient of a rare and spectacularly close encounter—except that I had seen none of it.

"There, behind you!" Gil was looking past me and pointing.

About ten feet behind me, the otter had stuck her head (I fancied calling it a "her") out of the water and was looking squarely in my direction. I let go of the side of the boat and, swimming very slowly while careful to keep my head above the surface, started breaststroking toward her. I had approached to within perhaps six feet when she suddenly vanished. Where had she gone? I heard Gil call out softly.

"Behind you! She's behind you."

I spun. The otter had indeed appeared directly behind me. I started toward her, and she disappeared again. A moment later Gil's voice sounded afresh. His enthusiasm had reached new levels. "She's behind you again." Was he laughing?

I turned, swam. The otter dived. It was plain now what was happening. She was playing with me.

Every time I started toward her, she would dive down and reappear behind me. It reached the point where I did not even have to start swimming. As soon as we made eye contact, she dove. Was she swimming around me, or under me? I found out moments later when, treading water forcefully, I kicked something with my right foot, hard. There was no mistaking what it was.

I immediately tensed. Had I hurt her? Would she vanish now—or interpret the kick as an attack and react offensively?

Seconds later, she popped up, staring at me. Clearly, I had not hurt her. I surmised that from an otter's standpoint my accidental kick was all part of the game.

This continued for nearly half an hour: me spinning in the dark water, her diving back and forth beneath me, until she finally grew tired of the diversion and swam off. I watched her depart, having burned every bit of adrenaline my body was capable of producing. We had interacted in her habitat for some thirty minutes without a hint of a hostile gesture on her part. She had bumped me several times; I had kicked her unintentionally and ungently. Why had she remained behind to play when the rest of her family had hastily departed as soon as I had entered the water? I thought I knew the answer.

She must be a teenager.

Surely, that was it. A wary cub would immediately have sought protection from the adults in the group. An adult would have departed in a more leisurely fashion or might possibly have reacted aggressively. But a young adult—teenagers are the same everywhere, with an innate curiosity and a zest for entertainment that transcends species. I have observed this trait in gorillas and elephants, in dolphins and sharks. I don't know for a fact that my playful friend was a juvenile, but she was certainly not full-grown. Any natural aggressiveness she might have possessed had been canceled out by a desire to amuse herself at the expense of the strange visitor to her watery world.

Sometimes in life we get lucky.

When told this story, those knowledgeable about the behavior of giant otters in the wild are united in their opinion that by entering their domain, I had taken a real chance. But if you want to experience that which is out of the ordinary, you have to take chances. Whether the object of your interest be giant otters, or big cats, or big fish, or big bugs, or tiny ants, if you want to understand them or get to know them more than just a little, you have to enter their realm. You cannot get this from television, or from movies, or even from reading.

Go. See. Touch. Listen, smell, and try to understand. And while you're learning, you are free to marvel at some of Nature's most exquisitely designed creatures. They may bite, they may sting, but you risk your life every time you cross the street or stand in a wet shower or bathtub. The rewards to be had from such potentially lethal everyday endeavors are miniscule compared to those to be gained from watching a leopard hunt or making eye contact with a shark, or from espying the ripple of color that is a snake retreating in haste into the depths of the rain forest.

Hearing or reading these stories, people sometimes ask me, "How can you do these things?"

To which my answer and explanation is and always will be:

"How can you not?"

CONCLUSION

BUT WHAT GOOD IS IT?

It's a question I'm often asked. What's the point of such encounters? Nearly being eaten, or stung, or bitten, or poisoned, being parasitized, risking not always replaceable parts of your body, and for what? What's the point? Why choose to voluntarily invite such experiences when one could be lounging on a beach in the Tuamotus, or strolling through the Prado, or ordering *schlag* with your coffee at an outside table at Demel?

The answer is that I've done those things, too: There's just not very much drama in them (well, maybe the bill at Demel). It's all grist for the writer's mill. The more so if you write fantasy or science fiction. I'm a firm believer that to create otherworldly settings you have to experience as much that's alien to your everyday life as possible. To invent other cultures you should immerse yourself in other cultures. In the old days, writers would attempt to do this by subscribing to *National Geographic* and by camping out in their local library. Today we have the Internet. But reading, in whatever format, is not the same as doing. Or as Robert Louis Stevenson put it, "Books are all right in their way, but they're a mighty poor substitute for life."

So how do I know when, where, and how I'm going to make use of experiences such as those I've related here? The answer is that I don't. What I *do* know is that sooner or later I'll be working on a story or a novel and a situation will arise involving a dramatic, perhaps potentially life-threatening confrontation. Often I'll produce the resulting scenario out of whole cloth, but sometimes—sometimes I'll think back to a situation from real life. Drawing on that will produce fiction that cannot help but be more realistic because the source of it has actually been experienced.

Oh, sure, you say. Like Air Jaws. Flying great white sharks. *That'll* prove useful in a story some day. Sure it will.

See the novel *Into the Thinking Kingdoms.*

Or how about interacting with a semi-wild cheetah named Felix, or encountering feeding lions? See all of the novels in the Journeys of the Catechist trilogy.

Years ago, I created an oversize otter character (Mudge, from the Spellsinger fantasy series) before I knew such a creature actually existed. Seeing his real analog only inspires me to write more about him. How about Pip, the flying snake from the Pip and Flinx books? Yes, I created her before I'd ever traveled outside the United States, but I firmly believe that subsequent serpentine encounters have enabled me to render her far more believably in later works than if I had never encountered her actual brethren in the wild. And it's not just individual creatures. That the description of the Amazon rain forest in *Phylogenesis* was singled out for especial compliment by one reviewer is due, I'm certain, solely to the fact that I've actually spent time there.

In *Blue Magic,* book one of the as yet unpublished Oshanurth trilogy, magic is commonplace, and much of it relates directly to the creatures that practice it. I refer, in particular, to shark magic, the basis of which lies entirely with the sharks that I've met. The octopus is there, too, along with dozens of other underwater denizens among whom I've spent some time.

Confront, encounter, interact with a creature, and you are made aware of the unique characteristics it may not share with other inhabitants of the planet. This holds true for plants as well as animals, as anyone who has read *Drowning World* or the *Midworld* stories will attest. The environment of *Drowning World* and much of the invented flora and fauna therein can be traced directly to time spent in the Amazon and, especially, in a reserve called Mamiraua that lies about halfway between Manaus and the Peruvian border.

I have to go now. A kitten is growling and nibbling on my toe. As a writer, I could extrapolate from her to full-grown cheetah or lion or tiger.

But it's better, much better, and far more fulfilling both professionally and as a human being to have encountered her family relations in person.

The End

CPSIA information can be obtained at www.ICGtesting.com
Printed in the USA
BVOW022245080412

287034BV00002B/2/P